1800 QUIPS
AND ILLUSTRATIONS
FOR ALL OCCASIONS

Prochnow Speaker's Library

1800 Quips and Illustrations for All Occasions
700 Illustrations and Ideas for Speakers
400 Illustrations for Ministers and Teachers
1000 Stories and Illustrations for All Occasions
1400 Ideas for Speakers and Toastmasters

1800 Quips
and Illustrations
for All Occasions

Herbert V. Prochnow

Baker Books

A Division of Baker Book House Co
Grand Rapids, Michigan 49516

Reprinted 1973, 1994 by Baker Books
a division of Baker Book House Company
P.O. Box 6287, Grand Rapids, MI 49516-6287

Previously published as *The Speaker's Source Book*

Printed in the United States of America

ISBN 0-8010-7146-1

PREFACE

This book is meant to be helpful to two groups of persons. First, it is meant for those who need a source of hundreds of stories, quips, and illustrations of all kinds from which they can select items that will be useful in introductions and speeches, and in committee meetings or other events related to social, civic, professional and business affairs. Second, this book is for those who like to read humorous, serious and inspiring stories and epigrams for their own enjoyment.

There are approximately 1,800 items in this book. They represent biographical, humorous and inspiring stories, striking facts and observations about life, as well as scores of quips and witticisms. The stories cover a broad range of interests. They include not only humorous and serious stories, but also many that are inspirational. Sometimes they give the observations of distinguished persons in various walks of life.

Having good stories and illustrations in mind can be helpful on many occasions. Stories can be used to make a point convincingly in discussion or to give an effective introduction of a speaker. With a slight change the same story can be adapted to many situations and uses. Whether one is presiding at a meeting, introducing a speaker, making a speech, giving a few casual remarks, or is merely engaged in discussion, the stories and witticisms in this book should prove useful.

Here is a book of stories, illustrations and epigrams for practical reference use or for enjoyment. The index should make the book easy to use.

Thomas Herbert

CONTENTS

CHAPTER 1

STORIES FROM BIOGRAPHY

Wisdom

When President Eliot of Harvard was asked how he accounted for his good health and vigorous mind at his advanced age (he was then 88, and lived 4 years longer) he included in his reply this significant phrase:

"A calm temperament expectant of good."

From Rivals to Partners

Baby elephants born in captivity are no longer a novelty, but many years ago when P. T. Barnum's Circus had a strong rival in the show of James A. Bailey, the birth of a baby elephant in the latter's menagerie became front page news. The cunning little creature, playful as a kitten, held the crowds enraptured. Barnum was pale green with envy. He sent a telegram to Bailey, inviting him to name his own price for the baby pachyderm. Bailey promptly wired back that Barnum didn't have money enough to buy the animal. Then Bailey published both telegrams in his show advertising.

A bit unethical, by modern standards, but it was shrewd advertising strategy. No one realized it more keenly than Barnum, the advertising wizard, who felt like kicking himself for thus playing into his rival's hands.

But his chagrin quickly gave way to the desire to have Bailey's wits working for the Barnum show, rather than against it. Presently he proposed to Bailey that they combine their rival enterprises into one grand, mammoth, unrivaled spectacle. So it was (thanks to a baby elephant) that the great Barnum & Bailey Circus was formed.—*Sunshine Magazine*

The Genius of Leonardo da Vinci

There was no highway of learning, that Leonardo da Vinci did not explore. He was perhaps the greatest and most successful engineer of his time, as well as the deepest thinker and most profound investigator into all the known branches of science of his age. Perhaps no more versatile genius has ever graced the earth—painter, and sculptor, musician, engineer, architect, inventor, philosopher, physicist, chemist, geologist, consummate director of state affairs and public functions. Any one of his brilliant gifts would have set him above all his fellows.

Leonardo was contemporary with Columbus. He was forty years old, at the height of his career, when the Genoan mapmaker was "sailing due west" in the effort to find a shortcut to India's fabulous riches. At sixty he had learned many of the principles of flying and was the first man to attempt to build a practical flying machine.

The dukes who hired Leonardo appreciated his skill as a military engineer even more than his genius with brush and chisel. He designed a horse-drawn "tank" which literally mowed down the enemy. Giant rotating blades projected from the front, rear, and sides. Another interesting weapon was a 12-barrel machine gun. He barely missed inventing the steam engine when he devised a huge steam cannon. The rear of the cannon barrel was heated red hot. Water injected into the barrel produced steam power sufficient to hurl a 79-pound projectile more than half a mile! He had already learned how to transform reciprocal motion into circular motion, so he had all the elements of the steam engine in his hands. How he failed to visualize it is hard to understand.

In the field of industrial science he invented the roller bearing, and a rolling mill for producing sheet metal. Until then, billets of metal were flattened by hammering. Hot Italian summers turned his fertile brain to devising an air-conditioning system, which employed the modern method of cooling the air by passing it through water spray. And, believe it or not, he worked on an "automobile," powered by the driver through differential gears!

A Civilian

During the Confederate attack on Fort Stevens, President Lincoln came out from the White House to make a tour of Union defenses. The task of piloting him fell to Oliver Wendell Holmes, aide-de-camp to the general in command. Lincoln wanted to know where the enemy were, and Holmes pointed them out. The President stood up to look. Standing, and supplemented by his high plug hat, Mr. Lincoln was a target of exceptional visibility, and there came a snarl of musketry fire. Grabbing the President by the arm, the young officer dragged him under cover, saying, "Get down, you fool!"

This was not the approved style for an officer to employ in addressing the commander-in-chief of the armed forces of his country. The youthful aide's relief from worry came when, just as Lincoln was quitting the fort, he took the trouble to walk back.

"Good-bye, Colonel Holmes," he said. "I'm glad to see you know how to talk to a civilian."

Trouble With Numbers

Albert Einstein arrived in London, carrying his violin. An old friend greeted him, then asked, "You still play the violin, Albert?"

The famous mathematician nodded, "Yes, but not very well. My teacher says, 'The trouble with you, Mr. Einstein, is that you can't count.' "

A Lifetime

During one's lifetime a person may be rated by the number who serve him, but after his passing he is measured by the number he served.

Napoleon made himself master of France and most of Europe by the power of his armies, but Louis Pasteur made himself the servant of France and the world in fighting the germs of disease.

Mussolini dominated Italy for a decade, and was dishonored. Signor Marconi put his electrical wizardry at the service of his nation and is still honored in the world's Hall of Fame.

The Communists go into the Congo to divide and dominate, while Albert Schweitzer devoted his life to healing the natives of Africa.

"Whosoever would be great among you let him be your servant."

Simple Things Are Often the Hardest

When Defoe wrote Robinson Crusoe, he did something as good artistically as Milton achieved in "Paradise Lost." Everybody is able to read Robinson Crusoe with pleasure and profit, but not one in ten thousand can master "Paradise Lost."

Yet the peculiar fact is that even those who have never read ten lines of "Paradise Lost" will give Milton a higher rank as an artist than Defoe. Writing that is simple, lucid, and understandable is usually considered inferior to that which is smothered by technique.

Tolstoi, the great Russian novelist, wrote:

"I can remember once speaking to a famous astronomer who had given public lectures on the spectrum analysis of the stars of the Milky Way, and saying it would be a good thing if, with his knowledge and masterly delivery, he would give a lecture merely on the formation and movements of the earth, for certainly there were many people at his lectures on the spectrum analysis of the Milky Way, especially among the women, who did not know why night follows day and summer follows winter. The wise astronomer smiled as he answered: 'Yes, it would be a good thing, but it would be very difficult. To lecture on the spectrum analysis of the Milky Way is far easier.'"

Punishment Enough

When Voltaire arrived in England in 1727, he found that feeling ran high against the French, that on the streets of London he was in grave peril. One day during a walk a crowd of angry citizens shouted, "Kill him! Hang the Frenchman!" Voltaire stopped, faced the crowd, and cried: "Englishmen! You want to kill me because I am a Frenchman! Am I not punished enough, in not being an Englishman?" The crowd cheered and provided him safe conduct back to his dwelling.

Was Aristotle Right?

Aristotle in 330 B.C. set down some curious observations regarding the effects of thought. The great philosopher declared that, barring physical defects, he could watch a man walking and tell whether that man's thoughts were about the future, the past, or the present.

He noted that young men habitually look upward; their thoughts are in the future. Middle-aged men look straight ahead; their thoughts are in the present. Old men look downward; their thoughts are in the past.

He asserted that the direction of one's gaze determined the orientation of that person's thoughts. If a man looks steadily upward, he will tend to think of the future. If he looks straight ahead, he will be concerned with the present. If he allows his gaze to rest on the ground, his thoughts will wander back along the path of memory.

The Admirable Crichton

James Crichton was probably the greatest prodigy that ever lived. He was born in 1560 in Scotland. At 13 he was given a college degree of bachelor of arts. At 17 he was given a master of arts. At 19 he went about Europe, challenging all the learned men to meet him in open forum. He boasted he could answer any question in any field of learning, speaking in any one of ten languages. He confronted his auditors not only with his remarkable knowledge but with the facility of his expression.

He was literally a human encyclopedia, knowing all about everything.

Not only did Crichton startle the world with his feats of mental agility, but he was equally proficient in nimbleness and strength of body.

He was a painter, a singer, a dancer, a horseman, a card-player—apparently equally skilled in all the social and fine arts.

One of his biographers called him "The Admirable Crichton," a sobriquet that has been written into literature, and now means a person who can turn his hand to just about anything.

Chrichton was killed at the age of 22 by a drunken prince whom he was employed to tutor.

The remarkable part of his career, and the point we wish to emphasize here, is that The Admirable Chrichton was as helpless as an inanimate library when it came to putting his vast knowledge to use. He accomplished no useful thing during his short life, and his biographers doubt whether a longer life would have made any difference. He invented nothing, he formulated no new theory, not a single noble thought bears his name. His mind was like the wax of a recording phonograph; it received impressions and reproduced what was recorded.

Mere learning serves no useful purpose. To be useful, a man must apply and interpret knowledge. This The Admirable Crichton, with all his book learning, could not effectively do. —*Sunshine Magazine*

A New Experience

Mark Twain was a guest at a Metropolitan Opera performance. His hostess kept up a running fire of comments and conversation throughout the arias—to his profound annoyance.

At the final curtain she turned to him and gushed, "You've been so grand a guest I want you to be with us again next Friday for 'Tosca.' "

"That will be interesting," said Sam Clemens. "I've never heard you in 'Tosca.' "

Michael Faraday

It was in the laboratory, so the story goes, of the great English physicist and chemist, Michael Faraday. An assistant had inadvertently dropped a silver cup into a jar of acid. The cup was nearly consumed before it was discovered, and before long was completely dissolved. The incident brought up a discussion about the indestructibility of matter. How could that theory be right, when here was a sizable chunk of silver completely disintegrated, not even a tiny pile of ashes or a streak of rust left to mark its place?

Faraday had a ready answer. Adding a chemical to the acid, the invisible silver was precipitated back into a solid. Retrieved and sent to a silversmith, it came back to the laboratory once more a silver cup. Nothing had been lost.

All matter, the scientists say, is like that. Nothing is ever lost. True, not everything that is "destroyed" can be restored to its original form. At least not yet. We can collect all the carbon, all the metal, all the other elements, but we cannot restore them in the form of the flower, the tree, the great painting they once were. We are not yet that intelligent and perhaps it is a good thing.

Nevertheless, nature's alchemy is constantly replacing that which has seemed to be wholly lost. A forest giant falls, decays, becomes dust. From that dust and decay rise new giants, taking their life and strength from the old.

Of Course

After making a name for himself in Denver journalism, Eugene Field, the humorist-poet, was offered a job on a Chicago newspaper. The editor suggested a two-year contract at $50 a week.

"I'll take $50 for the first year," said Field, "but I want 50c more for the second."

The editor looked at him questioningly.

"I just want people to know," explained Field, "that I'm on the way up."

St. Patrick

Patrick is, next to Nicholas, the most familiar of the post-biblical saints; but his actual life rivals that of Nicholas for obscurity. We can say with some assurance that he was (a) not a native Irishman; (b) not born on March 17; (c) not in any way a snake-charmer or a snake-eliminator; and (d) not buried under the granite slab which bears his name and lies in the shadow of Downpatrick Cathedral.

It is fairly certain that he was born in Wales about 389. The date of March 17 was set years after his death on little historical evidence. The story of his kidnapping by Irish marauders and his years as a shepherd in Connaught is on safer ground, but at that point he showed his opinion of Ireland by leaving it as soon as possible after his release. Following some travel and a stay at his home in Wales, he seems to have reached his great decision. He entered an abbey in France to seek ordination and to prepare himself specifically for service in Ireland.

His first Irish mission was to combat heresy among the small group of Christians there; but his activities soon went far beyond that. Starting a church in a barn at Saul in County Down (the location is still pointed out to visitors) he set out to convert the whole island. When he retired as Bishop of Armaugh some twenty years later he had just about succeeded. He found a pagan land and made it a part of Christian Europe. As long as men think of Ireland he will live in their hearts.—*Sunshine Magazine*

Sometimes the Door Isn't Locked

When Harry Houdini was building his reputation as an escape artist, he used a stunt to get a great deal of free publicity. He would visit the local jail and get the jailer to manacle him with everything he had in the way of handcuffs and straitjackets, then lock him in a cell. He was often back in the warden's office before that astonished gentleman had had time to hang up his hat.

Only once was he completely baffled. It was during a tour of Scotland. The jail was old, the lock antique, and he fully expected to be out of it in a matter of minutes, maybe seconds. He had no trouble shedding the manacles. Nothing but the cell door stood between him and freedom. But for once, he found a lock that would not yield. He tried everything he knew, finally working to the point of exhaustion.

At last, almost willing to admit himself licked, he leaned against the door to catch his breath. To his astonishment, the door creaked, then swung out on its rusty hinges. The canny old jailer, well aware that his locks were nothing to compare with those of Scotland Yard and other jails from which Houdini had escaped, had pulled a fast one. The door had not been locked at all!

Diplomacy

During a gala gathering in Springfield, Illinois, Abe Lincoln was asked by a young widow to guess her age. Lincoln was equal to the task.

"I have a good idea," he said, "but the big trouble is that I don't know whether to make you ten years older because of your brains or ten years younger on account of your looks."

Robert Fulton

Two hundred and four years ago, on November 14, 1765, Robert Fulton was born in Lancaster County, Pennsylvania. Although Fulton is best known as the inventor of the first practical steamboat, he began his career as an artist. Being more of a mechanic than an artist, Fulton spent more time studying the science of mechanics than he did in the study of art. While in Paris, Robert Fulton developed first a submarine and later a steamboat. Failing to interest Napoleon in his inventions, Fulton returned to the United States, where he built the first successful steamboat, the Clermont.

Who Said That?

Here are some common phrases used every day. See if you have any idea where they came from:

"Thanks for nothing."

"No limits but the sky."

"To give the devil his due."

"A peck of troubles."

"Let the worst come to the worst."

"A finger in every pie."

"Every dog has his day."

"A wild goose chase."

Give up? Every one of them appeared in one book, *Don Quixote*, written more than 350 years ago by Miguel de Cervantes.

He Himself Was Well

One day when John Quincy Adams was 80 years of age a friend met him on the streets of Boston. "How is John Quincy Adams?" this friend asked gaily. The old man's eyes began to twinkle, and then he spoke slowly: "John Quincy Adams himself is very well, thank you. But the house he lives in is sadly dilapidated. It is tottering on its foundations. The walls are badly shattered, and the roof is worn. The building trembles with every wind, and I think John Quincy Adams will have to move out before very long. But he himself is very well." and with a wave of his hand the old man walked on.

Sebastian S. Kresge

Sebastian S. Kresge was a short, stocky, sturdy Pennsylvania Dutchman who grew up in circumstances of poverty and by dint of his character, his wisdom, his insight and his faith developed one of the greatest mercantile empires in the United States. He retired as president of his company in 1925, but served as chairman of the board until he was ninety. From the time I first knew him I was greatly impressed by his calm, imperturbable character. No problem flustered Mr. Kresge, no circumstance agitated him. He would always say, "I think we can work this thing out if we don't get het up about it."

Kresge was a man of few words, and he did more good with his money than almost anybody I know of. His idea was that money was to be made to give away to make the world a better place in which to live; which is the Christian attitude toward money, if you ask me. Anything he had to say, he said simply. Harvard University gave him an honorary degree, and they asked him to make a speech after the degree had been conferred. There was a big audience sitting there prepared to listen to a speech on how he had lived a successful life. But he walked to the edge of the platform and just said, "I never made a dime talking." Then he sat down. They say it is by all odds the shortest speech ever made at Harvard; to my mind one of the most sensible also.—*Norman Vincent Peale*

Habit

I've played so many maid roles, when I go home, I usually walk in through the back door.—*Thelma Ritter*

Talent

Mary Martin is okay, if you happen to like talent.—*Ethel Merman*

Writers

I don't think it's a good idea for writers to fraternize with writers. It leads to a sort of inbreeding which in turn produces idiots.—*Somerset Maugham*

Fly Like Birds!

During the 1870s a bishop whose jurisdiction covered a small denominational college made his annual visit to the campus, and stayed with the president. During their conversation one night the bishop boasted a firm belief that everything that could be invented had been invented.

The college president thought otherwise. "Why, in fifty years," he asserted, "men will fly like birds."

The bishop was shocked. "Flight," he replied, "is reserved for angels. My dear man, you have been guilty of blasphemy."

The name of the bishop was Milton Wright; back home he had two small sons—Orville and Wilbur.

Immanual Kant

How often we hear a man condemn another with the critical observation, "Oh, he's in a rut!"

Ruts are not popular, yet they can be helpful as well as harmful—like habits, of which there are good and bad. The man bound more or less by a fixed routine of activity quite generally is apt to accomplish more than the man less restricted. There is greater chance of his effort being better organized and sustained. He doesn't have to stop to plan each move; he can proceed with his work without lost motion. Oriented in his tasks, he suffers no mental confusion.

In all history perhaps no man was more in a rut than Immanual Kant. For fifty years the great thinker and writer rose precisely at five o'clock every morning, and studied two hours —lectured the next two, and then wrote until noon, when he went to the same restaurant for his only meal of the day. Following that, he walked for an hour, rain or shine, timing himself closely, his servant always at a required distance behind him. Concluding this period of exercise and relaxation, he returned home, to read until bedtime.

In all those fifty years there was little or no variation in his day's program; he walked the same route and did the same things each day. From beginning to end, his life was a rut, yet he was one of the brilliant minds of the period—better informed than any contemporary, and a thinker whose influence extends into our generation.

A fixed routine can become extremely monotonous; but applying the right mental attitude makes the going easier, and the outcome safer.

His Answer

A prudish lady once accosted the learned Samuel Johnson shortly after publication of his monumental dictionary of the English language.

Said she, "Dr. Johnson, I am distressed that your dictionary contains so many vulgar words." Replied the gentleman, "Madam, I am immeasurably distressed that you actually looked them up!"

Onward Christian Soldiers

The words to the famous hymn, "Onward Christian Soldiers," were written in 1865 by the Reverend Sabine Baring-Gould for the church picnic. The minister believed a marching song would help keep the Sunday school children together. He and his assistants searched for an appropriate song, and when it could not be found, Baring-Gould sat up late into the night writing those words which he set to a Haydn tune. The tune most often used today was written for a new hymnal six years later by Sir Arthur Sullivan.

Advice

Once a man who had been slandered by a newspaper came to Edward Everett, asking what to do about it. Said Everett: "Do nothing! Half the people who bought the paper never saw the article. Half those who saw it, did not read it. Half those who read it, did not understand it. Half those who understood it, did not believe it. Half those who believed it are of no account anyway."

The Pursuit of Happiness

Although we speak of "the pursuit of happiness," as one of our rights, we all know that happiness seldom is captured by pursuing it. It comes as the result of pursuing other things. Chase after happiness and you'll never find it. But go after other things and happiness will find you!

Edison found happiness in the chase after new ideas. Burbank found it in the search for new varieties of plants. Paderewski found it in his hours of practice at the piano. John Muir found it by climbing mountains. Goethals found it by digging the Panama Canal.

Joseph Strauss found it by building the Golden Gate Bridge. Gutzon Borglum found it by carving the faces of great Americans on Mount Rushmore, in the Black Hills.

Some of man's biggest headaches came from directly pursuing happiness. And some of his truest happiness comes from apparently running away from it.

What Stradivari Did

Over 300 years ago, Antonio Stradivari made his famous Cremona violins whose quality has never been surpassed. He set a high standard of excellence for his workmanship.

Stradivari is credited with the authorship of the following specifications for making a perfect violin: "To carve a violin go to the Black Forest and cut out the heart of a tree 300 years old. Carry the wood to Greece and leave it there for 100 years, to absorb the eloquence of Athenian orators, to witness the tragedy of Grecian masters. Then take it to Italy for another 100 years. Saturate it with the greatness of ancient Rome.

"Thence to the White Cliffs of Dover for another 200 years. Let it take in the sweep of the tide, the flash of lightning, the rumble of heavy thunder and the rhythmic beat of the waves.

"On, for another 100 years to the newly built Palace of Versailles. Let it there absorb the gaiety of the night life, the dignity of the court, the majesty of its architecture. For another century to the mountains of Norway, to gather the clash of the avalanche, the sputter of waterfalls, the steady pulse of peasants.

"For the bow, take the hair of a woman who has loved and sinned and been to the foot of the cross for deliverance. Then you will have the violin and the bow. But only God can make the violinist."

Every fine product made is fashioned to an inspirational ideal. It is in striving for perfection that high levels of quality are achieved.—*Sunshine Magazine*

The Scientist

Perhaps as simple and yet profound a confession of faith as I have ever heard from a scientist's lips came from Dr. Robert

A. Millikan, California Institute of Technology. He has personally measured "e," the charge on the electron, and had hobnobbed with cosmic rays for years. In telling the fascinating story of cosmic rays to the scientists assembled, he finished by saying, "So, gentlemen, perhaps the Creator is still on the job."

Indeed, a Christian can be a scientist, and a scientist can be a Christian.—*The Free Methodist.*

Aesop's Fables

Of course you are acquainted with many of Aesop's fables. Have you ever wondered just who this famous storyteller was?

Aesop is supposed to have been a Greek slave who lived from 620 to 560 B.C. He had a brilliant mind, but an ugly, crippled body. This, however, did not prevent his becoming famous as a wise man who could teach moral lessons, in short pithy stories. So great did his reputation become that his master freed him, and he went to live at the court of Croesus, the famous and very rich King of Lydia. Once the King sent him to the temple of Apollo at Delphi and there he met his death, being thrown over a precipice by the angered inhabitants of that place.

Aesop told his stories by word of mouth, and they were handed down from one generation to another.

It Still Does

Back in 1776, James Watt advertised his newly invented steam engine in terms that miners would understand—horsepower. A horse walked 330 feet in one minute to hoist a 100-pound pail of coal, hence one horsepower equalled 33,000 foot pounds. It still does.

A Tribute To Lincoln

There is no new thing to be said of Lincoln. There is no new thing to be said of the mountains, or of the sea, or of the stars. The years go their way, but the same old mountains lift their granite shoulders above the drifting clouds, and the same mysterious sea beats upon the shore, and the same silent stars keep holy vigil above a tired world. But to mountain and sea and star, men turn forever in unwearied homage. And thus with Lincoln. For he was mountain in grandeur of spirit, he was sea in under-voice of mystic loneliness, he was star in steadfast purity of purpose and of service. And he, too, abides forever.

The years go their way, but with the name of Lincoln childhood still learns to voice a patriot's devotion, and with the name of Lincoln tears are called from old men's eyes. And there is no new thing to be said of him.

But while the Republic endures, upon whose altar he laid his great mind and heart, while liberty is cherished, while civic virtue and service and sacrifice are honored in the earth, the name of Lincoln will be spoken in undying love by the sons of men.—*Homer Hoch, a Justice of the Kansas Supreme Court*

Great Lessons

When the famed historian, Charles A. Beard, was asked if he could summarize the great lessons of history, he replied in four short sentences: 1. Whom the gods would destroy, they first make mad with power. 2. The mills of the gods grind slowly, but they grind exceedingly fine. 3. The bee fertilizes the flower it robs. 4. When it is dark enough, you can see the stars.

Instant Fun

A boat being towed on a trailer has this name: INSTANT FUN, and underneath these words: "Just add water."

Guarantee Satisfaction

When Woodrow Wilson was president of Princeton University, an anxious mother was questioning him closely about what Princeton could do for her son. Wilson replied: "Madam, we guarantee satisfaction or you will get your son back."

Epitaph

Thomas Jefferson composed the epitaph for his own grave. It read thus:

"Here was buried Thomas Jefferson, Author of the Declaration of American Independence, of the Statute of Virginia for Religious Freedom, and Father of the University of Virginia."

He neglected to mention that he was once President of the United States!

He Enjoyed the Course

When French poet Pierre Emmanuel taught at Harvard summer school a few years ago, students attended his lectures in droves. The administration was dismayed, however, when Emmanuel left for Paris at the end of the session without submitting grades for his students.

A cable was dispatched to him, and back came the poet's reply: "Give them all A's. I enjoyed the course."—*John J. McAleer, Boston Globe*

No Signature

Henry Ward Beecher, famous New England clergyman, was opening his mail one morning. Drawing a single sheet of paper from an envelope, he found written on it the one word: "Fool." The next Sunday, in the course of his sermon, he referred to it in these words: "I have known many an instance of a man writing letters and forgetting to sign his name. But this is the only instance I've ever known of a man signing his name and forgetting to write his letter."

Exit

Thomas Edison hated formal dinners, which seemed stuffy to him. One night at a particularly dull gathering, he decided to sneak away and return to his laboratory.

As he was pacing back and forth near the door, waiting for an opportune moment to escape, his host came up to him.

"It certainly is a delight to see you, Mr. Edison," he said. "What are you working on now?"

"My exit," replied the inventor.

No Easy Job

Returning from a trip to India, Mark Twain was describing his visit to a maharaja.

"He is surrounded by luxury," said Twain, "but he lives in constant fear of being poisoned. He has a salaried taster who samples every morsel of food that leaves the kitchen."

"Have many maharajas been lost as a result of poisoning?" the humorist was asked.

"No," said Twain, "but the tasters have thinned out appreciably."

Spiritual Message

Charles Malik of Lebanon said something that every American should read twice: "The trouble is that you in America, who have a great spiritual heritage, and a great spiritual message to give to the rest of the world, are not giving it." Surely, Mr. Malik is right. The most refrigerators, the largest bank accounts—these superlatives are important, but they are not the real foundation on which America is built. For a stronger America, we must lavish our attention on the roots and the vine of our system, rather than on its shiny fruits.—*Rev. A. Purnell Bailey, Grit*

Favorites

They tell in the folklore of Boston about the day Honey Fitz—former Mayor John F. Fitzgerald—was standing in the Custom House tower when a guide arrived with Hollanders desiring a panoramic view of the city. Honey Fitz saluted them cordially. "Ladies and gentlemen," he said, "Many years ago, when I was Burgomaster of Boston, the German people were among our best citizens."

At which point the guide whispered to the Mayor urgently: "Sir, they are Dutch."

No eye batted Honey Fitz. "But the Dutch," he continued suavely, "were my favorites."—*New York Times*

Men Descending From the Clouds

As far back as January 16, 1784, Ben Franklin foresaw and commented on the danger of "parachute troops." He had just witnessed successful balloon flights over the city of Paris, and on the date mentioned above he wrote to a friend in France: "It appears, as you observe, to be a discovery of great importance and what may possibly give a new turn to human affairs . . . Five thousand balloons, capable of raising two men each, could not cost more than five ships of the line, and where is the prince who can afford so to cover his country with troops for its defense, as that ten thousand men descending from the clouds might not in many places do an infinite deal of mischief, before a force could be brought together to repel them?"—*Sunshine Magazine*

Good Church Member

A horseman once went to Henry Ward Beecher, the great preacher, and said, "Mr. Beecher, I have a good family horse I want to sell you. He is a good saddle horse, a good buggy horse, and a good carriage horse. He works double with any other horse, one on either side of the tongue. In short, he is a good all-round horse and a good team worker."

Mr. Beecher replied, "My friend, I can't buy your horse, but I would like to have him as a member of my church."

Persistence

Audubon, the greatest of all bird painters, spent fifteen years in making sketches of birds, and left them in a trunk. When he went to look for them, he discovered that rats had nibbled his drawings to shreds.

Isaac Newton's dog tore a manuscript to pieces that had represented the work of a quarter of his lifetime.

A careless maid threw a huge manuscript by Thomas Carlyle into the fire.

But these men did not use their discouragement as a convenient excuse for giving up the fight. All of them went back to work and made another try for success.

Only One Best Place

One evening when Thomas Edison came home from work, his wife said to him, "You've worked long enough without a rest. You must go on a vacation."

"But where on earth would I go?" asked Mr. Edison.

"Just decide where you would rather be than anywhere else on earth," suggested his wife.

Mr. Edison hesitated. "Very well," he said finally, "I'll go tomorrow."

The next morning he was back at work in his laboratory.

Feeling the Weight

A visitor once wandered behind the scenes at Oberammergau before the presentation of the Passion Play, and saw among the props the cross leaning against a wall. He picked it up, and, staggering under its weight, asked, "Does it need to be so heavy?" Anton Lang, who played the part of the Christ, answered immediately, "I couldn't play the part unless I felt the weight." We often wonder why we are unconvincing as Christians, yet we can only be convincing if we, too, feel the weight of the burdens of the world.

Solo Performance

That evening's concert was the musical high spot of the winter in the small Nebraska college town. A student, working her way through, was bitterly disappointed when her job at the hotel desk kept her away. The evening dragged by. As her stint was almost over, there approaching the desk was the great artist herself. Had the girl attended the concert, she inquired? The forlorn youngster, somewhat overwhelmed, explained.

Then followed an unforgettable moment. In the hotel lobby, unaccompanied, contralto Marian Anderson sang for her the "Ave Maria."—*Sunshine Magazine*

The Way to Learn

George Gershwin did not sit around, waiting for inspiration to bring him good ideas. Oscar Levant, who lived with him for a long time, says Gershwin got most of his ideas just by playing. Whenever he sat down to the piano to amuse himself, something came of it. He looked upon his work as play. Creating his career was his way of having fun. His life was proof of the theory that the way to learn how to do anything is to do it.

George Washington

Many scoffers believe the story of George Washington and the cherry tree was a figment of the imagination of the Washington biographer Parson Weems. The Library of Congress has turned up the fact that a piece of German pottery—made ten years or more before Parson Weem's book was published in 1800—was decorated with the quaint illustration of the cherry tree story. It shows a youth in the clothing of the Continental period standing near a felled tree. Also shown is a large hatchet with the letters "G.W." and the numerals "1776." Whether true or not, apparently the story was current long before Parson Weems put it into his book.—*Sunshine Magazine*

To Get It Done

James Thurber, in Hollywood writing a screen version of his story, "The Catbird Seat," was assigned a secretary to dictate some dialog to. She protested: "I don't take dialog. Just letters."

Thurber found a way to overcome this. He introduced every scene with: "Dear Sam."

Fifth Best

The late Cedric Hardwicke liked the best of all his press notices one bestowed on him by George Bernard Shaw who wrote: "Hardwicke is my fifth favorite actor, the other four being the Marx brothers."

Washington's Rules of Conduct

George Washington learned the value of self-discipline at a very early age. While still a young boy he compiled a list of 101 Rules of Conduct which had a great influence on his life and became the foundation of his character. Here are a few choice excerpts from Washington's Rules of Conduct:

Sleep not when others speak, sit not when others stand, speak not when you should hold your peace, walk not when others stop.

Let your countenance be pleasant, but in serious matters let it be somewhat grave.

Show not yourself glad at the misfortune of another, though he were your enemy.

Let your discourse with men of business always be short and comprehensive.

Strive not with your superiors in argument, but always submit your judgment to others with modesty.

When a man does all he can, though it succeeds not well, blame not him that did it.

Associate yourself with men of good quality, if you esteem your own reputation, for it is better to be alone than in bad company.

Speak not injurious words, neither in jest nor earnest; scoff at none although they give occasion.

Be not forward, but friendly and courteous; the first to salute, hear, and answer; and be not pensive when it is a time to converse.

Think before you speak; pronounce not imperfectly, nor bring out your words too hastily, but orderly and distinctly.

Be not curious to know the affairs of others, neither approach to those that speak in private.

Undertake not what you cannot perform, but be careful to keep your promise.

Speak not evil of the absent, for it is unjust.

Labor to keep alive in your breast that little spark of celestial fire, called conscience.—*Sunshine Magazine*

No Friend

On one occasion John Barrymore was playing in a Broadway theatre, and there was a very noisy person in one of the boxes directing remarks to the stage to show that he knew Jack. Finally, Barrymore walked to the footlights, in the middle of a scene, and said, "Ladies and gentlemen, please excuse my friend in the box. I haven't seen him for a long time. Now you understand why!"

Home for Christmas

Orville and Wilbur Wright had tried repeatedly to fly a heavier-than-air craft. They had had one disappointment after another. Finally one December day, off the sand dunes of Kitty Hawk, they actually flew. It was the greatest news scoop of the century. Elated, they wired their sister Katherine, "We have actually flown one hundred twenty feet. Will be home for Christmas." Hastily she ran down the street and shoved the telegram at the city editor of the local paper. "Well, well," he smiled, "isn't it nice that they will be home for Christmas."

Message

If I could get just one message over to youth, it would be that it does not take genius to succeed in life. Any young man of ordinary intelligence who is morally sound, open and above-board in his dealings, not afraid of work, and who will play the game fairly and squarely, and keep everlastingly at it—should succeed in spite of obstacles and handicaps. Opportunity there must be—but usually it is neither great nor golden—just a little start or opening that serves only as a beginning.—*James Cash Penney, merchant and philanthropist*

George Bernard Shaw Observations

The liar's punishment is not in the least that he is not believed, but that he cannot believe anyone else.

The things most people want to know are usually none of their business.

A pessimist thinks everyone is as nasty as himself, and hates them for it.

Discovered Electricity

A student, asked to write a composition on Ben Franklin, wrote as follows:

"Benjamin Franklin was a poor boy. He went to Phila-delphia to live. He didn't have many clothes. One day he walked down the street and saw a pretty girl. She smiled at him; he smiled at her. Before long they were married and he discovered electricity."

Author

British Prime Minister Benjamin Disraeli was also a successful novelist. As a writer, he didn't think too highly of his contemporaries. On one occasion, he was asked if he had read a new novel by a leading author. "No," replied Disraeli. "When I want to read a new novel, I write one."—*Milwaukee Jounal*

Opinion

When Carl Sandburg attended a young playwright's dress rehearsal and fell asleep, the dramatist chided, "How could you sleep when you know how much I wanted your opinion?" Sandburg replied, "Young man, sleep is an opinion."

Shaw to Churchill

George Bernard Shaw once sent Winston Churchill two tickets to an opening night performance of his new play with the suggestion, "Bring a friend if you have one." Churchill's response was that he was otherwise engaged and requested tickets to the next performance, "if there is one."

Memory

Fiorello La Guardia, three time mayor of New York, was a man of quick temper. However, he was just as quick to forget what it was that caused him to flare up.

Once, in a fit of anger, he ordered two of his top officials to hand in their resignations in 24 hours. The officials, competent men, decided to ignore the order.

The 24 hours passed and they did not hear from the mayor. They did not, in fact, hear from him until six months had passed, when he informed them that they had been promoted.—*Milwaukee Journal*

He Doesn't Like Him

Ferruccio Tagliavinin, Italian tenor, on why he sang in Italian the lead roles of the "Pearl Fishers" in an opera at Philadelphia while the rest of the cast used French, native tongue of composer Georges Bizet: "I don't like de Gaulle."

Changed His Mind

About three o'clock one morning the telephone in Dr. Gallup's house rang. Sleepily the king of public opinion polls got out of bed and lifted the receiver.

"Is that Dr. Gallup?" asked the voice at the other end of the line.

"Yes, yes. What do you want?"

"I've just rung up to tell you I've changed my mind."

Heartwarming Answer

The Reverend Henry Ward Beecher, on a very cold day, stopped to buy a newspaper from a ragged youngster who stood shivering on a corner. "Poor little fellow," he said "aren't you cold standing there?"

The boy looked up with a smile and said, "I was, sir, before you passed."

The Solution of God

Shortly before his tragic death, Mr. Dag Hammarskjold, the Secretary General of the United Nations, was chatting with Billy Graham. Looking across the New York skyline and thinking of nations on the rim of the world, Mr. Hammarskjold said to Billy: "I see no hope for permanent world peace; we have tried so hard and failed so miserably." Then he said in a voice that Billy could hardly hear, "Unless the world has a spiritual rebirth within the next few years, civilization is doomed."—*Dr. Robert Lamont*

Poverty

The great Mozart, unable to afford heat in his room, wrapped his hands in woolen socks while writing some of his most immortal music. This great musical genius was first buried in a pauper's grave.

The Misplaced Letter

When, on the death of President McKinley, Theodore Roosevelt succeeded to the high office, a New York editor desired to contrast the event with a recent event in Europe. But the compositor, coming to the word "oath" in the manuscript, struck a wrong key and the sentence appeared: "For sheer democratic dignity, nothing could exceed the moment when, surrounded by the Cabinet, Mr. Roosevelt took his simple bath as President of the United States."

Speech

There are dozens of ways of squashing a heckler. . . . Sir Winston Churchill once turned to a particularly persistent heckler and remarked icily: "I might get angry . . . that is, if I valued your opinion."—*Nicholas Holmes, Weekend, England*

Wire Instructions

Robert Benchley, the humorist, was sent to Venice, Italy, to write an article about that city for a magazine.

The day after his arrival, the editor received a cable from him: "Streets under water," it read. "Wire instructions."

CHAPTER 2

STORIES OF INSPIRATION

Living the Christmas Spirit

Are you willing to stoop down and consider the needs and desires of little children;

To remember the weakness, the loneliness of people who are growing old;

To stop asking how much your friends love you and ask yourself whether you love them enough;

To bear in mind the things that other people have to bear in their hearts;

To try to understand what those who live in the same house with you really want, without waiting for them to tell you.

Then you can keep Christmas.

And if you keep it for a day, why not always?

But you can never keep it alone.—*Henry Van Dyke*

The Little Room

Before the United States Supreme Court moved into its sumptuous eleven-million-dollar marble temple a few years ago, it carried on its work in a comparatively small room in the Capitol building. The members of the Court were understandably elated by the move—all except one. Justice Brandeis said he would have preferred to have the Court continue in its earlier quarters, because "our little room kept us humble." Would the decisions handed down by the Supreme Court in recent years have been different if that august body had remained in the "little room?"

Friendship

As to the value of other things most men differ, concerning friendship all have the same opinion. What can be more foolish than, when men are possessed of great influence by their wealth, power, and resources, to procure other things which are bought by money—horses, slaves, rich apparel, costly vases—and not to procure friends, the most valuable and fairest furniture of life? And yet every man can tell how many goats or sheep he possesses, but not how many friends. In the choice, moreover, of a dog or of a horse, we exercise the greatest care: we inquire into its pedigree, its training, and character, and yet we too often leave the selection of our friends, which is of infinitely greater importance—by whom our whole life will be more or less influenced either for good or evil—almost to chance.—
Cicero

Bear It in Mind

Drop a stone into the water—
In a moment it is gone,
But there are a hundred ripples
Circling on and on and on.
Say an unkind word this moment—
In a moment it is gone,
But there are a hundred ripples
Circling on and on and on.
Say a word of cheer and splendor—
In a moment it is gone,
But there are a hundred ripples
Circling on and on and on.

Not the Brush

A young artist, who was studying under a great master, came one day to the studio to beg for permission to use his master's brush. The request was granted, and with a singing heart the young man went away to his own painting, thinking that now his work would be much better.

A short while later he returned with the brush, complaining that he could do no better with it than he could with his own. An assistant in the studio, hearing the young man's complaint, said to him, "Friend, it is not the master's brush you need, but the master's devotion, the master's spirit."

Michelangelo's Pieta

This great sculpture represents two life-sized figures. Jesus, who has just been taken down from the cross, rests peacefully on the lap of his mother. Mary, portrayed as still a very young woman, hand outstretched, gazes down at the Crucified, who is now sleeping peacefully. The whole is intended to convey the sorrow or pity (hence the name Pieta) which a mother had for her Son.

Peter Pan

In Kensington Gardens in London there stands the bronze statue of Peter Pan. Around the pedestal on which he stands are his friends, the rabbits, a snail, fairies and rats, a hare and a serious old rook. If you should chance to see the statue as the sun begins to sink in the west, you will see the little animals have heads and backs, not of bronze, but (as it seems) of gold. These little creatures are highly polished because of the loving hands that have caressed them before turning away from Never Never Land into a world governed by clocks and customs.

A Useful Idea

That great practical man of science, Thomas A. Edison, once gave a young man this advice: "Make it a habit to keep on the lookout for novel and interesting ideas that others have used successfully. Your idea needs to be original only in its adaptation to the problem you are working on."

A Mother's Favorite Children

Starting research for a book in which he planned to show the misery resulting from large families, a sociologist interviewed the mother of thirteen children. After taking down information about the children's ages, family income, and such, he asked, "Do you think all children deserve the full, impartial love and attention of a mother?"

"Of course," she said.

"Well, which of your children do you love the most?" he asked, hoping to catch her in a contradiction.

"The one who is sick until he gets well," she answered, "and the one who is away until he gets home."

Worry

What to do with worries: "I don't see how you could bear the sorrow you've known in your lifetime," the visitor sympathized.

"The Lord bore it for me," her friend said.

"Yes," said the visitor, "we must take our troubles to the Lord."

"We must do more than that," replied her friend. "We must leave them there. Most people take their burdens to Him, but they bring them away with them, and are just as worried and unhappy as ever. But I take mine and I leave them with Him, and come away and forget them. And if the worry comes back, I take it to Him again; and I do this over and over, until at last I just forget I have any worries, and am at perfect rest."—*Hannah Whitall Smith in Lutheran Digest*

Stay Young

Stay young by taking inspiration from the young in spirit who remained creatively active all their lives: Goethe completing Faust at 80; Titian painting masterpieces at 98; Toscanini conducting at 85; Justice Holmes writing Supreme Court decisions at 90; Edison busy in his laboratory at 84; Benjamin Franklin helping to frame the American Constitution at 80.

Growing Old

Marcus Tullius Cicero, in the year 136 B.C. tells his friend Cato his happy experience in growing old.

In De Senectute (concerning old age) he expresses this philosophy:

"It is delightful to have the consciousness of life well spent and the memory of deeds worthily performed and of blessings personally acquired, but it is even more satisfying to retain the love of intellectual adventure.

"I am in my eighty-fourth year. So you see, old age has not quite enfeebled me or broken me down; the senate house does not miss my strength, nor the rostra, nor my friends, nor my clients or my guests. For I have never agreed to that old and much-praised proverb which advises you to become an old man early if you wish to be an old man long. I, for my part, would rather be an old man for a shorter length of time than be an old man before I was one.

"Life's race-course is fixed; Nature has only a single path and that path is run but once, and to each stage of existence has been alloted its own appropriate quality; so that the weakness of childhood, the impetuosity of youth, the seriousness of middle age, the maturity of old age . . . each bears some of Nature's fruit, which must be garnered in its own season. Each has something which ought to be enjoyed in its own time.

"We must make a stand against old age, and its faults must be atoned for by activity. We must fight, as it were, against disease, and in a like manner against old age. Regard must be paid to health, moderate exercise must be adopted; so much of meat and drink must be taken that the strength may be recruited, not oppressed. Nor, indeed, must the body alone be supported, but the mind and soul much more; for these also, unless you drop oil on them as on a lamp, are extinguished by old age—our minds are rendered buoyant by exercise.

"As I like a young man in whom there is something of the old, so I like an old man in whom there is something of the young; and he who follows this maxim will possibly be an old man in mind.

"Intelligence, reflection and judgment reside in old men . . . Age, especially an honored old age, has so great authority that this is of more value than all the pleasures of youth . . .

"Old age is the consummation of life, just as of a play. It is rich in blessings.

"Remember, too, to those who have NOT the means within themselves of a virtuous and happy life, every age is burdensome."

Whom Do You Worship?

The story goes that one Sunday Henry Ward Beecher had to be absent from Plymouth church, and his brother preached for him. The church auditorium was crowded, but when it was evident that the eloquent Henry Ward Beecher was not going to appear, many started to leave the church.

The brother of the great man was not disturbed. Calling for silence, he said, "All who came this morning to worship Henry Ward Beecher may leave now. The rest will remain to worship God." No one left after that.

The Adventurous Life

The only life worth living is the adventurous life. Of such a life the dominant characteristic is that it is unafraid. In the first place, it is unafraid of what other people think. Like Columbus, it dares not only to assert a belief but to live it in the face of contrary opinion. It does not adapt either its place or its objectives to the pace and objectives of its neighbors. It is not afraid of dreaming dreams that have no practical meaning. It thinks its own thoughts, it reads its own books, it develops its own hobbies, it is governed by its own conscience. The herd may graze where it pleases or stampede when it pleases, but he who lives the adventurous life will remain unafraid when he finds himself alone.—*Raymond B. Fosdick*

A Calculated Risk

"There is a calculated risk in everything. There has been a calculated risk in every stage of American development. The nation was built by men who took risks—pioneers who were not afraid of the wilderness, businessmen who were not afraid of failure, scientists who were not afraid of the truth, thinkers who were not afraid of progress, dreamers who were not afraid of action.—*Brooks Atkinson*

A Single Life

Norman Cousins, editor of *The Saturday Review of Literature,* in an article entitled "Confrontation," spoke of the discouraging impact that the way of life in Southeast Asia has upon American newcomers. The aura of romance fades quickly when they gaze upon a people perpetually hungry; men harnessed to wagons; twelve people living in one room; many sleeping on the streets.

Accustomed to abundance and luxury, many Americans become afflicted by "compassion fatigue." "Why help one man when there are fifty others standing in line behind him? It's no use!" said a young American with an American Agricultural Mission. An expert in housing was defeated and frustrated, for the population grows faster than houses can be constructed. A young doctor in India wondered why he struggled to keep a baby alive who had nothing to look forward to except sickness and hunger.

Cousins confesses that an immediate, far-reaching result cannot be expected from the many programs of assistance designed by Americans to improve the living conditions of people in many underprivileged sectors of the world. "But that is no excuse. To help put meaning into a single life is the best kind of individual responsibility."

Let Us Not Forget

"Let it never be forgotten that glamor is not greatness; applause is not fame; prominence is not eminence. The man of the hour is not apt to be the man of the ages. A stone may sparkle, but that does not make it a diamond; a man may have money but that does not make him a success. It is what the unimportant do that really counts and determines the course of history. The greatest forces in the universe are never spectacular. Summer showers are more effective than hurricanes, but they get no publicity. The world would soon die but for the fidelity, loyalty, and consecration of those whose names are unhonored and unsung."—*Dr. John R. Sizoo*

Contented Living

Nine requisites for contented living: Health enough to make work a pleasure; wealthy enough to support your needs; strength enough to battle with difficulties; grace enough to confess your sins and overcome them; patience enough to toil until some good is accomplished; charity enough to see some good in your neighbor; love enough to make you to be useful and helpful to others; faith enough to make real the things of God; hope enough to remove all anxious fear concerning the future.—*Johann Wolfgang von Goethe (1749-1832)*

Tension

The story is told of Thomas Carlyle that when he lived in London he was much annoyed by a pet rooster which belonged to a neighbor and had a rather unfortunate habit of practicing his vocal lesson at odd hours of the night, invariably awaking Carlyle from his sleep. Finally he protested to the owner of the bird, who was extremely sorry for the annoyance, but said he was quite sure his rooster did not crow more than three or four times a night, and some nights not at all. "That may be true," replied Carlyle, "but if only you could know what I go through while waiting for him to crow!"—*Reverend William E. Phifer Jr., D.D., Christian Observer*

Lincoln Stories

Lincoln once criticized a Greek history for its tediousness, and a diplomat took him to task about it. "The author of that history, Mr. President," he said, "is one of the most profound scholars of the age. No man of our generation has plunged more deeply into the sacred fount of learning."

"Yes, or come up drier," said Lincoln.

* * *

When asked to give his opinion of General Philip Sheridan, who had just taken command of cavalry under General Grant, Lincoln replied, "He is one of those long-armed fellows with short legs who can scratch his shins without having to stoop over."

* * *

Lincoln liked to joke about superstitions. "Look at this," he said one day, taking a potato from his pocket. Asked why he carried it, he replied: "For rheumatism. I haven't had a twinge of rheumatism since I've been carrying it." A by-stander exclaimed, "Wonderful!" "Yes," said Lincoln. "And still more wonderful is the fact that it's retroactive, too. I never had a twinge before I began carrying it, either."

Lincoln, then a young lawyer, and a judge were bantering about horse trading. They agreed to swap, with $25 to go to the shrewder dealer. At the appointed hour the judge arrived with the sorriest nag imaginable. Lincoln came along a few minutes later with a wooden saw horse on his shoulders. Amid laughter Lincoln set down his "horse" and commented, "Well, judge, this is the first time I ever got the worst of it in a horse trade."

Your Destiny

I don't know what your destiny will be, but one thing I know: the only ones among you who will be really happy are those who have sought and found how to serve.

—*Albert Schweitzer*

The Common Man

The Common Man dogma may be of use as a vote-getting device. It supposedly proves the humility of the demagogues. The humor of it is that when we get sick, we want the uncommon doctor. When we go to war, we yearn for the uncommon general or admiral. When we choose the president of a university, we want an uncommon educator. The imperative need of this nation at all times is the leadership of the Uncomman men and women. We need men and women who cannot be intimidated, who are not concerned with applause meters, not those who sell tomorrow for cheers today.—*Herbert Hoover*

The True Joy

This is the true joy of life—the being used for a purpose recognized by yourself as a mighty one, the being thoroughly worn out before you are thrown to the scrap-heap; the being a force of nature instead of a feverish, selfish clod of ailments and grievances.—*George Bernard Shaw*

When the Day Is Dark

When the day is dark and gloomy
And the fog obscures your view,
And you feel there is no challenge
Waiting anywhere for you;
When it's routine you must follow
Through a dreary weather chart,
And you feel the hand of duty
Like a millstone on your heart;
Face the skies however darkened,
When you ache to turn away
Do the job that lies before you,
Keep your courage one more day.
You can never guess how often
You affect another's life
By the fact you are a doer
Not a quitter in the strife.

—*Auther Unknown in a Worden & Risberg Leaflet*

A Letter From Christian Missionaries in the Middle East

Sometimes God crosses our lives with others in such an emphatic way that we cannot avoid it. Surely—because it happened kamaan. (Arabic work for "again.")

This time we were on the way from Jerico to Jerusalem, traveling that same road as the "good Samaritan." Instead of a trail it was a black-topped double lane. Instead of a donkey it was a Volkswagen at 80 kilometers per hour. Instead of evening it was near midnight.

The VW's lights cut a path of visibility down the road. Then, as a car approached us with terribly bright lights, it erased that path. We could see only a short distance ahead—and there, before us at 80 kilometers per hour, was a stone barricade two to three feet high. We had the choice of the approaching car, the stones, or the dark ditch to the right. I chose the rocks.

We flew over the top—bent the fender and bumper, slashed the right tire, bent the hub and front axle, and put holes through the trunk and pan. We ground to a stop. The approaching car roared by. I don't know if the priest or Levite was driving it. Another car came along, slowed, and stopped. Three rough-looking characters jumped out, two of them carrying long guns tucked into their belts. I thought for a moment that the thieves of the Good Samaritan story had made their appearance. Instead, they turned out to be the "Good Samaritans."

They took over, using the tools of their used car business to put my car back into running condition. For better than an hour, they crawled under that car—working the stubborn jack and cursing it, hammering the hub and axle and cursing it, dirtying their clothes and cursing them. And when they were finished and the car could run, with a smile they said goodbye. To offer to pay them would have been impossible. Instead, they invited us to be their guests when traveling through Amman and insisted that we take their address along with their names.

As their tail-lights disappeared, I thought: By their language—the vulgarity and curses—they were not Christians. By their names—Mahoud, Mohammad, and Muath—they were not Christians. But that didn't seem to be the question. The question was, "Who had been the neighbor to us?" and the answer was, "He that showed mercy to us." (Luke 10)

"Ka-maan!" It had happened "Kamaan," hadn't it? God had crossed our lives with people who have made an impression on it. It was emphatic and it was thrilling. Our prayers have been that our lives in this place have had an impression on others.

Lord, make us neighbors to those around us.—*Missionaries Dennis and Ellen, Denell and Eric Hilgendorf*

Lighting the Candle

More than 100,000 spectators taught themselves an unforgettable lesson when they jammed the Los Angeles Coliseum one evening. They had gathered to watch a mighty pageant honoring the city's war heroes. After a mock battle scene had driven home the seeming helplessness of the human individual, silence fell. Only the voice of the master of ceremonies could be heard.

He began in a clear, resonant voice; "Perhaps you sometimes say to yourself, 'My job isn't important because it is such a little job.' but you are wrong. The most obscure person can be very important. Let me show you what I mean," he said, raising his hand for a signal.

The giant searchlights, bathing every corner of the great Coliseum, were shut off, transforming the daylight splendor of the arena into total darkness.

Then the speaker struck a match, and in the blackness the tiny flame could be seen by all.

"Now you can see the importance of one little light," said the master of ceremonies. "Suppose we all strike a light."

Instantly matches were struck all over the stadium until nearly 100,000 pinpoints of light illuminated the summer night. Everyone gasped with surprise. Quickly and effectively they comprehended that it is within the power of each single individual to "light a candle" instead of "curse the darkness."

—Christopher News Notes

Self-Reliance

What I must do is all that concerns me, not what the people think. This rule, equally arduous in actual and in intellectual life, may serve for the whole distinction between greatness and meanness. It is the harder because you will always find those who think they know what is your duty better than you know it. It is easy in the world to live after the world's opinion; it is easy in solitude to live after our own; but the great man is he who in the midst of the crowd keeps with perfect sweetness the independence of solitude.—*Ralph Waldo Emerson*

Fulfillment

I have worked in the fertile earth and planted a garden— so I know what faith is. I have listened to the birds caroling in the early morning and at dusk, so I know what music is. I have seen the morning without clouds after showers, so I know what beauty is.

I have sat before a wood fire with old friends, so I know what companionship is. I have walked the paths of quietness along the forest floor, so I know what peace is. I have dwelt in the valley of remembrance and on the hills of home, so I know what love is. I have seen the miracle of Spring, the fruition of Summer, and the beauty of Autumn, followed by the repose of Winter—so I know what life is. And because I have perceived all these things, I know what God is.—*Walter Lewis Smith, New York, in Praying Hands*

Faith

If our faith were simple like that of little children we would have less anxiety. One little girl expressed her utmost confidence in God by praying, "Dear God, please take care of yourself or we are all sunk." One child said to another, "Do you suppose that God gets cold at night up in heaven?" The other child replied, "No, silly. He pulls the clouds over Him."

A Rule of Life

Over the entrance to an old cathedral in France, these words stand out clearly: "He who bringeth no gift to the altar, beareth no blessing away." It is a rule for the worshipper; it is a rule for all of life.

When we go into the classroom, we must take the gift of attention, the discipline of study, the joy of work well done, the enthusiasm of an earnest searcher if we would bear the blessings of an education away with us.

When we go to a concert, we must take the gift of appreciation, understanding, deep feeling, and a desire for the best if we would carry the blessing of real art away with us.

When we go into a friendship, we must take the art of understanding, the joy of making another happy, the skill of objectivity, the power of versatility, if we would carry the blessing of a growing friendship away with us.

In other words, we can receive only by giving. It is one of the great rules of living.—*The Broadcaster*

Sincerity

The first virtue of all really great men is that they are sincere. They eradicate hypocrisy from their hearts. They bravely unveil their weaknesses, their doubts, their defects. They are courageous. They boldly ride a-tilt against prejudices. No civil, moral, nor immoral power overawes them. They love their fellow men profoundly. They are generous. They allow their hearts to expand. They have compassion for all forms of suffering. Pity is the very foundation-stone of genius.—*Anatole France, French Novelist*

Belief

A missionary in Africa, translating the Gospel of St. John into Songhai, couldn't find a word to express "believe." He took his problem to a native Christian. The dark man thought a few minutes and then suggested, "Doesn't it mean to 'hear in my heart?' "—*Sunday School World*

Little Things Count

We should mind little things—little courtesies in life, little matters of personal appearance, little extravagances, little minutes of wasted time, little details in our work. And it seems that a thing cannot be too small to command our attention.

The first hint Newton had leading to his important optical discoveries originated from a child's soap bubble.

The telescope was the outcome of a boy's amusement with two glasses in his father's shop.

Goodyear neglected his skillet until it was red hot, and the accident led him to the making of vulcanized rubber.

Little things! Yet how important they proved to be to the men who had the wish to correlate these little things with the ideas in their heads.—*O'Bannon's Between Calls*

The Minorities

It is always the minorities that hold the key to progress; it is always through those who are unafraid to be different that advance comes to human society.—*Raymond Blaine Fosdick*

Autumn

Some of us call it Autumn,
Others call it God.—*Wm. Herbert Carruth*

Thoughts

Thoughts are actual things. If a man indulges in evil thinking, he will find himself the victim of evil deeds. The man who covets, will be tempted to steal. The man who hates, will be tempted to destroy. In nothing do we employ greater wisdom or folly than in the discipline we use to control our thoughts, for every secret thought tends to become an outward act.
—*Sunshine Magazine*

Small Margin

It has been pointed out that success is built on small margins. The fastest runner in the world is only 5% faster than scores of ordinary runners. The difference between a great race horse and a good race horse is only a few seconds. Small differences in personality separate the superior salesman from the average. And that extra hour in the laboratory may make the difference in the lifetime search of a scientist.

Dare!

Thackeray wrote: "Let the man who has to make his fortune in life remember this maxim—attacking is the only secret. Dare, and the world will always yield. If it beats you sometimes, dare it again and again, and it will succumb."

Keep Your Eye on the Goal

The snow covered the ground and three lads were playing. A man said to them, "Would you like to try a race and the winner receive a prize?"

The boys agreed and the man told them that his race was to be different. "I will go to the other side of the field," he said, "and when I give you the signal, you will start to run. The one whose footsteps are the straightest in the snow will be the winner."

The race commenced and the first boy kept looking at his feet to see if his steps were straight. The second lad kept looking at his companions to see what they were doing; but the third boy just ran on with his eyes steadfastly fixed on the man on the other side of the field.

The third boy was the winner, for his footsteps were straight in the snow. He had kept his eyes on the goal ahead of him.

A Scientist's Beliefs

I believe:

That the power of God is complete,

That the authority of God is absolute and final,

That God is both Creator and Redeemer,

That in His providence, God is in control of his creation, and that He rules in the affairs of men, and that for this, Christ is His instrument and our contact,

That God is just (yet I do not always understand),

That God is loving, for He has provided a way through Jesus Christ so that by commitment to Him we may meet God's requirements and be acceptable to Him,

That the Bible, as the revealed Word of God, is the supreme authority for my faith and life.—*Dr. Elmer W. Engstrom, President, Radio Corporation of America*

Advice to a Young Man

I would say to you to work and live in such a manner as to be able to serve others, to plan so as to be able to advance something, to achieve so as to leave the world a little better than you found it—and, finally, to garner for yourself as much peace of mind, which is happiness, as you can.—*David Sarnoff*

Gordon Cooper's Prayer

As the world now knows, Gordon Cooper composed a prayer while rocketing in orbit around the world. Here's his prayer, as recorded while in orbit and as reported to Congress:

"Father, thank You, especially for letting me fly this flight. Thank You for the privilege of being able to be in this position; to be up in this wondrous place, seeing all these many startling, wonderful things that You have created.

"Help guide and direct all of us that we may shape our lives to be much better Christians, trying to help one another, and to work with one another rather than fighting and bickering.

"Help us to complete this mission successfully. Help us in our future space endeavors that we may show the world that a democracy can compete, and still be able to do things in a big way, and be able to do research development, and conduct many scientific and very technical programs.

"Be with all our families. Give them guidance and encouragement, and let them know that everything will be OK.

"We ask in Thy name. Amen."

Tests of Greatness

These are tests of true greatness: To bear up under loss; to fight the bitterness of defeat and the weakness of grief; to be a victor over anger; to smile when tears are close; to resist disease and evil men and base instincts; to hate hate and to love love; to go on when it would seem good to die; to seek ever the glory and the dream; to look up with unquenchable faith to something ever more about to be—these things any man can do, and so be great.—*Zane Grey*

Religion

Two California gold miners were on their way east with their nuggets. They came one evening to a hut and asked to stay the night. Their host gave them a room, but they were fearful that he might rob them while they slept so they agreed to take turns and keep on guard. After a while, the man assigned to the first watch stretched out to sleep. His companion awakened and protested that his watch was not over. "It is all right, Bill," said the man. "We can both sleep for the old man read the Bible and prayed. I saw him through a crack in the door."—*Bishop Gerald Kennedy, "The Starting Line," Pulpit Digest*

Religion

The late Glenn Frank once said that if we were to talk about our religious interests in the same normal matter-of-fact manner that we speak of our business affairs, we could start a revival of religion in America in a few weeks. When we grasp the truth all our business is a part of our Heavenly Father's business, we no longer rate some occupations as secular and others as sacred; we no longer treat our work as a hand-to-mouth existence, but we raise it to man-to-God nobility . . . To a godless person work is just a job. To a godly man work, however humble, is a vocation.—*Dr. Ralph W. Sockman*

Be Careful

A woman said, "My husband goes down to his store on Sunday mornings. I can't get him out of the store." Her pastor replied, "Tell him to be careful. He was born a human; he may die a grocer."—*J. B. Dengis, Sunday School Times*

A Source of Strength

I sought for the greatness and genius of America in fertile fields and boundless forests; it was not there. I sought for it in her free schools and her institutions of learning; it was not there. I sought for it in her matchless constitution and democratic congress; it was not there. Not until I went to the churches of America and found them aflame for righteousness did I understand the greatness and genius of America. America is great because America is good. When America ceases to be good, America will cease to be great.—*Alexis de Tocqueville, Democracy in America*

Christmas Still Lives

Volcanoes—earthquakes—floods—wars cannot destroy it; the darkness of fear cannot blot out its light; hatred, envy, and jealousy cannot withstand it; greed and selfishness retreat before it; nothing can stop its onward march into the hearts of men. Like a blanket of softly falling snow the spirit of Christmas covers the world! Once again a Babe is King; once again faith and love and service are abroad in the land! Christmas still lives!
—*Wilferd Peterson*

Thanksgiving

I urge all citizens to make this Thanksgiving not merely a holiday from their labors, but rather a day of contemplations. I ask the head of each family to recount to his children the story of the first New England Thanksgiving, thus to impress upon future generations the heritage of this nation born in toil, in danger, in purpose, and in the conviction that right and justice and freedom can through man's efforts persevere and come to fruition with the blessing of God.

Let us observe this day with reverence and with prayer that will rekindle in us the will and show us the way not only to preserve our blessings, but also to extend them to the four corners of the earth. Let us by our example, as well as by our material aid, assist all peoples of all nations who are striving to achieve a better life in freedom.—*John F. Kennedy's first Thanksgiving Proclamation of 1961*

Freedom and Self-Respect

When an American says that he loves his country, he means not only that he loves the New England hills, the prairies glistening in the sun, the wide and rising plains, the great mountains and the sea. He means that he loves an inner air, an inner light in which freedom lives and in which a man can draw the breath of self-respect.—*Adlai Stevenson*

Just Thinking

I am reminded daily, in my relationships with people, of what Clarence Francis said. It has always seemed to me that you can buy a man's time; you can buy a man's physical presence in a given place; you can even buy a measured number of skilled muscular motions per hour or day. But you cannot buy a man's initiative, nor his loyalty. Nor can you buy the devotion of hearts, minds and souls. You have to earn such things.—*Sir Oracle*

Freedom

Freedom is like a coin. It has the word "privilege" on one side and "responsibility" on the other. It does not have privilege on both sides. There are too many today who want everything in privilege but refuse to accept anything that approaches the sense of responsibility.—*Joseph R. Sizoo*

The Great Tragedy

"The great tragedy of life," said Somerset Maugham, "is not that men perish, but that they cease to love." It does not matter who or what one loves. What is important is that one desires to give one's self to some person or cause—to be willing, if necessary, to give life itself so that what one loves might have life.

The Ways

To every man there openeth
A Way, and Ways, and a Way,
And the High Soul climbs the High Way,
And the Low Soul gropes the Low,
And in between on the misty flats
The rest drift to and fro.
But to every man there openeth
A High Way and a Low,
And every man decideth
The Way his soul shall go.

—*John Oxenham (1861- 1941)*

Thoughts for Thanksgiving Day

The worship most acceptable to God comes from a thankful and cheerful heart.—*Plutarch*

The private and personal blessings we enjoy, the blessings of immunity, safeguard, liberty, and integrity, deserve the thanksgiving of a whole life.—*Jeremy Taylor*

Pride slays thanksgiving, but an humble mind is the soil out of which thanks naturally grow.—*Henry Ward Beecher*

A grateful thought toward Heaven is of itself a prayer. —*Gotthold Lessing*

O Lord, who lends me life, lend me a heart replete with thankfulness.—*Shakespeare*

If only I have the will to be grateful, I am so.—*Seneca*

He enjoys much who is thankful for little; a grateful mind is both a great and happy mind.—*Thomas Secker*

A thankful heart is not only the greatest virtue, but the parent of all the other virtues.—*Cicero*

Living Philosophy

As a child I believed that God created me. But now I understand that He not only created me as I was, but as I am and how I have developed. He created my ideals, my character, my abilities—such as they are—and my drive; and He created my property and my ability to hang onto some of it.

Now I would be an ingrate if in return for all of this I did not want to give something to my God. This is not necessarily religion. It's common courtesy; good manners, if you will. And so, in the things I do, I try to say thank you. The child says thank you with his mouth. The man says thank you with his actions; and there are degrees of action, just as there are degrees of understanding.

I did not come to this conclusion without a struggle, and I did not come to it alone. I have been helped by several people, and I have not always cooperated. My mother taught me my early faith. Years later, a great pastor raised my sights above the crowd and gave me the perspective of a greater height. My wife was not only willing but eager to put up with the sacrifice that this philosophy demands; and she had the good sense not to push me. I have been helped by a number of fine laymen with whom I have had the privilege to work, and whose standard of performance has given me something to reach for.

Nor did this philosophy develop overnight. At first, I grudgingly thought that a little work for my church would be enough. Later, when I was making more money, I thought that I could do it with dollars. But I was dead wrong. I had forgotten a significant sentence from Christ's Sermon on the Mount: "For where your treasure is, there will your heart be also." And then things really started to move.

In a nut-shell, for what God has given me, I want to give something in return to Him. I want to put more into this world than I take out, and to leave it richer than I found it.—*Brainerd Chapman of Pritchard, Chapman, Pennington, Montgomery and Sloan, from a talk before Sunday Evening Club, Chicago*

Poverty of WHAT?

Newspapers and magazines have been filled with articles about the war on poverty. But it seems that these analysts think of poverty only in terms of money income. The government is trying to provide income of a certain amount in the belief that, with material poverty obliterated, the individual can have all the good things in life and live happily ever after.

The popular impression seems to be that the individual cannot amount to anything in the world if he is poor financially. Apparently it has been forgotten that the great of the world have climbed to the heights from the hovels, half-starved, perhaps, but undeterred from the things they desired.

That is where our modern thinking stumbles.

The pages of history reveal great actors, writers, lawyers, artists, ministers, politicians—the list is endless. They were poor. They were hungry. But they achieved because they were rich in many ways.

We need to change our viewpoint. It is well to clean up the slums. It is well to try to find work for people who will work. It is a wonderful thing to provide an education for people who want it. But let us not mislead ourselves. Those who are poor in worldly goods will not be stopped if they are rich in character, moral fiber, courage, and ambition. They will develop the talent God has given them and nothing will stop them.

I do not mean that everyone has the divine spark of greatness. But any individual can help himself become a responsible desirable citizen—not rich, but with enough—honest and law-abiding if he so desires.

Even the Great Master himself was so poor that he told his friends, "The Son of Man hath not where to lay his head." But his words have endured for two thousand years, his life an example of wealth of spirit, of courage, of character.—*Donna Thompson, The Freeman*

His Lucky Day

David, a seven-year-old, was bumped on the bus going to school one day and suffered a two-inch cut in one cheek. At recess, he collided with another boy and two teeth were knocked loose. But life was inviting to David, so noon found him sliding on the ice where he fell and broke an arm.

David's parents rushed him to a hospital. Enroute, David attracted his father's attention by the way he was clutching something in his good hand. Upon questioning, he opened his hand and revealed a quarter.

"I found it on the ground when I fell," David said. "It's the first money I ever found. Dad, this sure is my lucky day!"

Famous Inscriptions

Over one of the doors of the Milan cathedral is sculptured a cross beneath which are the words: "All that troubles is but for a moment." Under the great central entrance in the main aisle is the inscription: "That only is important which is eternal."

Hope

An old man surprised everyone with his cheerfulness since he seemed to have an unusual amount of trouble and relatively few pleasures. When asked the secret of his cheery disposition, he replied, "Well, you see, it's like this. The Bible says often, 'And it came to pass,' never, 'It came to stay.' "

A Privilege

One of the most merciful and gracious privileges of humanity is the second chance, a new opportunity to rise triumphantly above any failures or defeats of the past.

Thanksgiving

Here is a holiday that commemorates no hero, celebrates no battlefield. No lobby is behind it; no group or sect or party. It doesn't even fall on the same date twice. Yet Christmas cannot dim it nor July 4th steal its glory. And all America loves it with a quiet and intense affection that is reserved for no other day of the year.

What makes Thanksgiving different? What makes it beloved? What makes it real?

Perhaps the answer is simple: Thanksgiving is an affirmation. It is our heart's testimony to a deeply held conviction— the conviction that these things we call free and decent and American did not just happen to us. We did not get them because we were wiser, or more clever, or even luckier.

This conviction is the sum of many beliefs and experiences. The belief in the dignity of every human being. The belief in a real right and wrong. The belief in decency and honesty and integrity. The belief in a responsibility, under God, to our fellow man, wherever he may be.

For these beliefs, and the American way of life, Thanksgiving Day is our joyous affirmation to a kind Providence for His blessings and guidance.—*Adapted from Titmus Tidings in Sunshine Magazine*

Shed No Tears

Shed no tears over your lack of early advantages. No really great man ever had any advantages that he himself did not create.—*Elbert Hubbard*

Prayers a Man Lives

The prayers a man lives on his feet are just as important as those he says on his knees.

Commencement

I once heard it said that a commencement speech should be aimed halfway between student and faculty, thereby assuring, I assume, a perfect miss. Whether the aim is poor or whatever the reason, after long experience with commencement orations I have concluded that they don't—or at least mine don't—communicate much of enduring value at this watershed in your lives when you pass from the brief interval of academic education to the long interval of education by action and experience.

I said to the students at Princeton once upon a time that "the laws, the aphorisms, the generalizations, the universal truths, the parables and the old saws—all of the observations about life which can be communicated handily in ready verbal packages—are as well known to a man at 20 who has been attentive as to a man at 50.

"What he knows at 50 that he did not know at 20 boils down to something like this: the knowledge he has acquired with age is not the knowledge of formulas, or forms of words, but of people, places, actions—a knowledge not gained by words but by touch, sight, sound, victories, failures, sleeplessness, devotion, love—the human experiences and emotions of this earth; and perhaps, too, a little faith and a little reverence for the things you cannot see."

64

My feeling of inadequacy on these occasions brings to mind Samuel Butler's remark when he was once asked to talk about how to make the most out of life. I think his reply was: "I don't even know how to make the most out of the next 15 minutes." And I feel that way about the next 20 minutes.

But, happily, your merciful president has not asked me to enlighten and inspire you with profound philosophy and luminous wisdom, but to talk a little about the role of educated Americans and the desirability of knowing more and more about the peoples and problems of other lands—the people in the other houses of this little village we call the world, if I can put it that way.

And so I will, because to know more—I was about to say "something"—about the world has become a condition of survival. By survival I don't mean only from violent death, but rather from the slow, lingering extinction of all we Americans are and mean as a people. In this age of seething revolution—political, scientific and ideological—the race is to the swift and wise and ready, and we must look to those who have enjoyed the privilege of some education to be swift and wise and ready.
—*Adlai E. Stevenson, Commencement Michigan State University*

Quotations Attributed to Benjamin Franklin

They that can give up essential liberty to obtain a little temporary safety deserve neither liberty nor safety.

What is serving God? 'Tis doing good to man.
God helps them that help themselves.
There never was a good war or a bad peace.
It is hard for an empty sack to stand upright.

Doing an injury puts you below your enemy; revenging one makes you but even with him; forgiving it sets you above him.

In this world nothing is certain but death and taxes.

It's Time to Stand Up for the Upperdog

I have just about reached the end of my tolerance for the way our society at the present time seems to have sympathetic concern for the misfit, the pervert, the drug addict, the drifter, the ne'er-do-well, the maladjusted, the chronic criminal, the underachiever, the loser—in general, the underdog.

It seems to me we have lost touch with reality and become warped in our attachments, if not in fact psychotic.

In short, I feel it is time for someone like me to stand up and say, "I'm for the upperdog!" I'm also for the achiever—the one who sets out to do something and does it; the one who recognizes the problems and opportunities at hand and endeavors to deal with them; the one who is successful at his immediate task because he is not worrying about someone else's failings; the one who doesn't consider it "square" to be constantly looking for more to do, who isn't always rationalizing why he shouldn't be doing what he is doing; the one, in short, who carries the work of his part of the world squarely on his shoulders.

Not the wealthy, necessarily; not the ones in authority, necessarily; not the gifted, necessarily—just the doer, the achiever—regardless of his status, his opulence, his native endowment.

We are not born equal; we are born unequal. And the talented are no more responsible for their talents than the underprivileged for their plight. The measure of each should be by what he does with his inherited position.—*Dr. Miller Upton*

The Christmas Tree

A favorite legend of the Germans infers that Christ selected the pine for the Christmas tree. The story relates that on the day that Christ was born, three trees—an olive, a date, and a pine—gathered around the manger to do homage to their Lord. The olive made an offering of its fruit and the palm its dates.

But the pine had nothing to give and was very sad. The great stars above looked down and were so sorry for the pine that they came down and rested on its branches. Then the Christ Child looked at the radiantly lighted tree and liked it best of all.

In Poland the Good Stars are praised as the bringers of the Christmas tree. In Hungary children thank the blessed angels for the trees. Some religious writers trace the origin of the tree back to Adam and Eve. Their contention is that December 24 has long been consecrated to Adam and Eve. Old almanacs uphold this statement. Furthermore, according to legend, Adam, on leaving the Garden of Eden, brought with him a cutting from the Tree of Knowledge. This, it is said, was planted and became not only the first Christmas tree, but also the wood of the cross on which Christ was crucified.

A final legend also comes from the North. It credits the first Christmas tre to Martin Luther.

The story goes that one starry Christmas Eve Martin Luther was returning home through the snow-clad forest. So impressed was he with the beauty of the trees and with the radiance of night that he cut an attractive little fir which he brought home with him. This he hung with candles; then. calling his children to him, he explained that as these little lights were to the greater stars, so all the lights of heaven and earth were to the Supreme Light above the sky.

That, say the followers of Luther, was the Christmas tree that started the Christmas tree custom that has brought so much happiness to young and old, all the world over.—*The Davey Bulletin*

The Penalty of Leadership

In every field of human endeavor, he that is first must perpetually live in the white light of publicity. Whether the leadership be vested in a man or in a manufactured product, emulation and envy are ever at work. In art, in literature, in music, in industry, the reward and the punishment are always the same. The reward is widespread recognition; the punishment, fierce denial and detraction. When a man's work becomes a standard for the whole world, it also becomes a target for the shafts of the envious few. If his work be merely mediocre, he will be left severely alone—if he achieves a masterpiece, it will set a million tongues a-wagging.

Jealousy does not protrude its forked tongue at the artist who produces a commonplace painting. Whatsoever you write, or paint, or play, or sing, or build, no one will strive to surpass or to slander you, unless your work be stamped with the seal of genius. Long, long after a great work or a good work has been done, those who are disappointed or envious continue to cry out that it cannot be done. Spiteful little voices in the domain of art were raised against our own Whistler as a mountebank, long after the big world had acclaimed him its greatest artistic genius. Multitudes flocked to Bayreuth to worship at the musical shrine of Wagner, while the little group of those whom he had dethroned and displaced argued angrily that he was no musician at all.,

The little world continued to protest that Fulton could never build a steamboat, while the big world flocked to the river banks to see his boat steam by. The leader is assailed because he is a leader, and the effort to equal him is merely added proof of that leadership. Failing to equal or to excel, the follower seeks to depreciate and to destroy—but only confirms once more the superiority of that which he strives to supplant.

There is nothing new in this. It is as old as the world and as old as the human passions—envy, fear, greed, ambition, and the desire to surpass. And it all avails nothing. If the leader truly leads, he remains — the leader. Master-poet, master-painter, master-workman, each in his turn is assailed, and each holds his laurels through the ages. That which is good or great makes itself known, no matter how loud the clamor of denial. That which deserves to live—lives.—*Written by Theodore F. Mac-*

Manus, as an advertisement in 1915, for Cadillac Motor Car Company

Character

Reputation is what men and women think of us; character is what God and the angels know of us.—*Thomas Paine*

For Your Birthday

May the road rise up to meet you,
May the wind be always at your back,
And may God hold you
In the hollow of His hand.—*Old Irish Blessing*

Just Thinking

We do not need more national development, we neeed more spiritual development. We do not need more intellectual power, we need more spiritual power. We do not need more knowledge, we need more character. We do not need more law, we need more religion. We do not need more of the things that are seen, we need more of the things that are unseen.—*Calvin Coolidge*

The Other Side

As the little girl tripped along at her father's side on an evening walk, she kept looking up at the stars. Though apparently fascinated, she made no comment. Finally her father asked what she was thinking about.

"If the bottom side of Heaven is so beautiful," replied the child, "how wonderful the other side must be."—*W. E. Golden*

Enemies

Blessed are my enemies, for they tell me the truth when my friends flatter me.

Blessed are my enemies, for they prevent all men speaking well of me.

Blessed are my enemies, for they tell me what they don't like in me, rather than the things they do like.

Blessed are my enemies, for they provide an object of love outside the small circle of my selfishness.

Blessed are my enemies, for they rub off the artificial varnish and make me see my natural complexion.

Blessed are my enemies, for their mirror of biting sarcasm and scathing rebuke reveals me to myself.—*Anonymous*

An Ancient Irish Prayer

May the blessing of light be upon you, light without and light within. May the blessed sunlight shine upon you and warm your heart till it glows like a great peat fire, so that the stranger may come and warm himself by it, and also a friend.

And may the light shine out of the two eyes of you like a candle set in two windows of a house, bidding the wanderer come out of the storm.

And may the blessing of the rain be upon you—the soft sweet rain. May it fall upon your spirit so that all the little flowers may spring up, and shed their sweetness on the air.

And may the blessing of the great rains be on you, may they beat upon your spirit and wash it fair and clean, and leave there many a shining pool where the blue of heaven shines reflected, and sometimes a star.

And may the blessings of the earth be on you—the great and round earth. May you ever have a kindly greeting for those you pass as you're going along the roads.

May the earth be soft under you when you lie upon it, tired at the end of the day. And may it rest easy over you when at the last you lie out under it. May it rest so lightly over you that your soul may be quickly through it, and on its way to God.

Motherhood

A mother was suddenly called out of town to nurse an ailing relative for a rather indefinite period. She left her husband and children to run the house. After a while, she began to wonder whether she was missed. All doubts were removed, however, by a letter from her youngest son. "Dear Mother," it read "Since you went away, this is the biggest house I ever saw."

A Promising Future

"First is the danger, given our present strength, that we may rest on our oars, thinking that the race is won. Actually, we may be only at the beginning of unexampled scientific and engineering achievement, on the threshold of an Augustan age of unparalleled creativity. With the future so promising, this is not the time to relax our scientific effort or for timid talk about having reached some kind of ceiling in our upsurge of scientific and technological strength."—*Dr. James R. Killian, Jr., Chairman, Massachusetts Institute of Technology*

Easily Recognized

Sir Bartle Frere was once on his way to visit a Scottish home. The master of the household, sending a servant to meet him, sought some description by which the visitor might easily be recognized. He said at last to the servant, "When the train comes in, you will see a tall gentleman helping somebody."
—*Sunshine Magazine*

The Cause of Mankind

"You can't sink half a ship," is a phrase that has been used in many an intragroup argument. Let us not forget that the human race today is in one and the same ship. Yet there are all too many persons—men of wide experience and apparent intelligence—who are focusing all their brain power along the lines of how to sink half of it. "Our cause," as Ben Franklin said in Paris in 1777, "is the cause of all mankind."—*American Appraisal Company*

God Is Awake

Have courage for the great sorrows of life and patience for the small ones; and when you have laboriously accomplished your daily task, go to sleep in peace. God is awake.—*Victor Hugo*

Business

Many a successful businessman and woman have succeeded less because of abilities which can be measured—academic abilities—than because of stick-to-itiveness and moral stamina, which so far we have no way of measuring.—*Joseph H. Morrow*

The Only Worthy Goal

The barbarian, the outlaw, the bandit are symbols of a civilization that is either primitive or decadent. As men grow in wisdom, they recognize that might does not make right; that true liberty is freedom under law; and that the arrogance of power is a pitiful substitute for justice and equity.

Hence once again we say to those in the Kremlin who boast of the superiority of their system: "Let us compete in peace, and let our course of action be such that the choice we offer uncommitted peoples is not a choice between progress and reaction, between high civilization and a return to barbarism, between the rule of law and the rule of force."

In a context of justice, of concern for the millions of men and women who yearn for peace, of a constant striving to bring the wealth abounding in this earth to those who today languish in hunger and want—in such a context, competition between the Communist world and the Free World would indeed be meaningful. Then we could say without hesitation: let the stronger system win, knowing that both systems would be moving in a direction of a world of peace, with increasing material prosperity serving as a foundation for a flowering of the human spirit.

We could then put aside the hatred and distrust of the past and work for a better world. Our goal will be peace. Our instrument for achieving peace will be law and justice. Our hope will be that, under these conditions, the vast energies now devoted to weapons of war will instead be used to clothe, house, and feed the entire world. This is the only goal worthy of our aspirations. Competing in this way, nobody will lose, and mankind will gain.—*Richard M. Nixon*

Death

If we truly realized the inevitability of death, we would be kinder and more helpful to our loved ones while they lived, for we should realize how precious is the passing moment of life.—*Faith Forsyte, Tit-Bits, London*

Thankful

A 7-year-old boy was walking home from Sunday School with his father. Without looking up he said, "Daddy, why don't we thank God for the things we don't have to have but we get them anyway?"—*The Reverend Don Jennings, Prairie Farmer*

Listening With the Heart

The story is told of a woman who during the war went to live with her husband in camp on the Mojave Desert in New Mexico. She simply hated the place; the heat was almost unbearable, 125 degrees in the shade, the wind blew incessantly, and there was sand—sand everywhere.

Finally, in desperation she wrote her parents in Ohio that she couldn't stand it another minute and was coming home.

Quickly came the reply by airmail from her father—just the two familiar lines:

"Two men looked out from prison bars,
One saw mud, the other saw stars."

The daughter did some real thinking, not only with the intellect but also with her heart. She decided to stick to her post. She made friends with the natives, learned to love the country, and eventually wrote a book about it. The desert hadn't changed, but her attitude had. Because she listened with her heart to the words her father sent, a whole new world opened up to her.—*Sunshine Magazine*

Decision

You don't achieve adulthood by letting others make all your decisions for you. Freedom is opportunity to make decisions. Character is ability to make right decisions. It can be achieved only in a climate of freedom. For no one learns to make right decisions without being free to make wrong ones. As our American freedoms keep diminishing, so does the character of our people.—*Reverend Kenneth W. Sollitt*

Persistence

There are two significant characteristics of every great life. The first is capacity to make a good beginning and the second is courage to push on to a good ending. One of the saddest things in life is to see a man begin some worthy venture revealing great promise and then to watch him flounder into failure for lack of courage to push on through frustration and disappointment. There is no easy road to achievement or to Christian character. . . . A life of triumph hinges on a firm faith for rugged times.—*Harold Blake Walker, Chicago Tribune*

Values

If you think you cannot do very much, and that the little you can do is of no value, think of these things: A teakettle singing on a stove was the beginning of the steam engine. A shirt waving on the clothes line was the beginning of a balloon, the forerunner of the Graf Zeppelin. A spider web strung across a garden path suggested the suspension bridge. A lantern swinging in a tower was the beginning of a pendulum. An apple falling from a tree was the cause of discovering the law of gravitation.
—*Forbes, Benjamin P. Forbes Co.*

Peace May Finally Reign

I stepped outside of the house, away from the noisy, happy festivities inside, and a great calm came over me. Here was the glory of God in the starlit night; the reflection of the moon in the lake; the whispering winds in the soft pines; the gentle chomping of the deer under the apple tree. Here was peace! The hunters were gone. The animals were unafraid. As I looked about, I wondered if it would be too idealistic to pray that some day the hunters of man, too, would go, and let the dove of peace really reign!—*Dr. Alfred P. Haake*

The Forgotten Man

Who is the Forgotten Man? He is that individual who does an honest day's work, pays his bills, brings up two or more children, keeps up a small savings account, never asks for charity from anyone, never gets into trouble with the police, never finds fault unless a principle is involved—in short, he is the individual who keeps going on his own momentum, good times, bad times, or indifferent times.

When the hat is passed around, the Forgotten Man chips in his mite. The taxgatherer visits him regularly, and collects toll for the upkeep of the police courts, jails, workhouses, and the relief rolls—none of which the Forgotten Man ever uses. He is self-supporting, self-starting, self-sufficient, and being so, he is counted in on nothing except the census.

The Forgotten Man is just the everyday, common, ordinary, plain citizen who does the best he can and makes a pretty good job of it. He is the man you can count on in times of war or in times of peace, in times of hysterical prosperity or in times of gloomy depression; in times of Republican management or in times of Democratic management. He is the dependable old horse, broken to harness, and he will stand without hitching.

Remember, there are millions of him, and there isn't much chance that he will ever go crazy even though the whole world about him does seem inclined that way. When things get too bad he will take a hand at running them himself, and you can depend upon him to do it in a sensible way.—*Sunshine Magazine*

Making Men

If I can make men of my people, my business will take care of itself. Everything I can do to help them ultimately benefits me. The more money I spend on them, the more enthusiasm they will have for my interests, and the more money they will make for both of us.—*Henry Ford*

Finest Human Qualities

The world will never have lasting peace so long as men reserve for war the finest human qualities. Peace, no less than war, requires idealism and self-sacrifice, and a righteous and dynamic faith.—*John Foster Dulles*

Confidence and Faith

I believe that if you think about disaster, you will get it. Brood about death and you hasten your demise. Think positively and masterfully, with confidence and faith, and life becomes more secure, more fraught with action, richer in achievement and experience.—*Eddie Rickenbacker*

State of Mind

State of mind is a very important factor in success because you can condition your mind to a point where it enables or prevents you from going forward and doing things. You can poison your own mind and limit your own capacity.—*David Sarnoff*

CHAPTER 3

HUMOROUS STORIES

But He Did

Nero's mother is reported to have said it after watching her son take his violin lesson: "That boy will never set the town on fire."

Optimist

An optimist is a man who can hand his car over to a parking-lot attendant without looking back.

I Remain

One of the shortest letters on record was written by a New York renter in response to his landlord's notice to vacate the house at once. Aware of his rights under state regulations, the renter replied: "Sir: I remain, Yours truly."

A Dead Circus

The teacher had taken her pupils for a trip through the Museum of Natural History.

"Well, Elmer," asked father when the boy returned, "where did you go with your teacher this afternoon?"

"Huh," replied Elmer with disdain, "we went to a dead circus."

Loses Something

James Thurber encountered a lady at a cocktail party who told him that his books were even funnier in French. "Ah yes," sighed Thurber, 'I lose something in the original."

Confident

A lawyer, whose eloquence was of the "spread-eagle" sort, was addressing a jury at great length when his legal opponent, growing weary, went outside to rest.

"Old Ironsides is making a great speech," someone said to him.

"Old Ironsides always makes a great speech," said the other. "If you or I had to announce that two and two make four, we'd blurt it right out. But Old Ironsides would say:

" 'If, by that particular arithmetical rule known as addition, we desired to arrive at the sum of two integers added to two integers, we should find—and I assert this boldly, sir, and without fear of successful contradiction—we, I repeat, should find by the particular arithmetical formula before mentioned—and, sir, I hold myself perfectly responsible for the assertion that I am about to make—that the sum of the two given integers added to the two other integers would be four.' "

Wonderful

Husband: "The bank has returned your check."

Wife: "Isn't that just wonderful! What shall we buy with it this time?"

Bachelor

The bachelor's a cagey guy who has a lot of fun; he sizes all the women up and never Mrs. one.

The Least He Could Do

The conductor of the community orchestra was almost out of his mind because at every rehearsal at least one member would be missing. At the last rehearsal, he called for attention and said, "I wish to thank the first violinist for being the only member of the orchestra to attend every rehearsal."

"It seemed the least I could do," the violinist said humbly, "since I won't be at the concert tonight."

Now Don't Doze

When it freezes and bloze, take care of your noze that it doesn't get froze, and wrap up your toze in warm woolen hoze. This advice, goodness knowze, was written in proze by someone who knowze the effect of cold snowze on your noze and your toze.

Impediment

Two men were discussing a mutual acquaintance. "Nice fellow," said one, "but have you noticed how he always lets his friends pick up the dinner bill?"

"Yes," replied the other. "He has a terrible impediment in his reach."

Couldn't Be Worse

School teacher: "Not only is he the worst behaved child in my class, but he also has a perfect attendance record."

In Trouble

Some railroad laborers who worked near a golf course were intrigued by the game. They saw a golfer knock the ball into a rut and have a hard time extricating it. Then he got into a sand trap and well nigh failed to get the ball out. At length he got a good shot and the ball trickled directly into the cup . . . whereupon one laborer who had watched the previous difficulties commented sympathetically: "Now, Mister, you're really in a fix!"

He Didn't Understand

Junior, who had just obtained a job with a big company, asked his grandfather if he had ever had to be careful lest he "bend, fold, or mutilate" his IBM personnel card. Grandpa wanted to know what an IBM card was. When Junior told him, Grandpa said he probably would have sweat the card through, and Junior wanted to know what that was.

Her Fault

There was a terrible crash as the train struck the car. A few seconds later, a man and woman crawled out of the wreckage. The woman opened her mouth to speak but the man stopped her. "Don't say a word," he snapped. "I got my half of the car across. You were driving in the back seat, and if you let it get hit it's no fault of mine."

The Real Difference

The real difference between a beautiful woman and a charming woman: A beautiful woman is a woman you notice, while a charming woman is one who notices you.

Capitalism

A distinguished Hungarian economist, just returned from a visit to the U.S. met a friend in a cafe. "What did you study in the U.S.?" asked the friend. "I went to study the death of capitalism," replied the economist. The friend then asked: "How did you find it?" Replied the economist with a sigh: "What a wonderful way to die."

Hard Problem

At an oil company's annual stockholders' meeting, one of the ladies present raised her hand. "Mr. Chairman, one thing has always bothered me ever since I bought stock in this company. When you build a new gas station on the street corner, how do you know you'll find oil?"

No More Bargains

A shrewd businessman, on a trip through the Southwest, spotted an Indian with a pile of blankets for sale.

"A hundred dollars for the lot," said the Indian.

"Twenty-four dollars," was the businessman's reply.

"Listen," said the Indian, "bargains like Manhattan Island you ain't going to get no more."

Pretty Bad Corn

"Hey, Larry, who's the father of all corn?"

"I give up."

"Popcorn, of course!"

Just Right

A man gave his chauffeur a box of cigars for Christmas. Afterwards he asked Sam how he liked the cigars. The chauffeur answered, "Those cigars were just right. If they were any better you wouldn't have given them to me, and if they were any worse I couldn't have smoked 'em."

He Could Hear Him

An after-dinner speaker had been going strong for 10 or 15 minutes when from the back of the room, someone shouted "louder!"

A man seated in front stood up and remarked, "I'll trade places with you; I can hear him."

Who Won?

When an American runner beat a Russian in a track event in which only the two of them participated, the sports writer for the Russian paper did not know how to report the result without admitting the Russian defeat. His editor had had more experience. He simply wrote: "Ivan came in second, but the American was next to last."

He's In Trouble

The young lady eyed her escort with great disapproval. "That's the fourth time you've gone back for more ice cream and cake, Albert," she said acidly. "Doesn't it embarrass you at all?"

"Why should it?" the hungry fellow shrugged. "I keep telling them I'm getting it for you."

Big Market Ahead

In St. Paul, Minnesota, a barber has come up with a solution for his bald customers. He has a new tonic that contains alum and lemon. He tells them, "It doesn't grow hair. It shrinks your head, so that what hair you have fits better."

Art Objects

A cynical-minded man was standing in front of an exhibit of modernism, labeled "Art Objects."

"Well," he announced to the attendant, "I can't say I blame Art for objectin'."

Smart Lad

A scoutmaster, after watching several new scouts at their attempts at outdoor cooking, asked, "How are you managing, lads? Have you forgotten any essential equipment?"

"Yes, I have," answered one of the scouts.

"Oh, what?"

"My mother."

Housewife

The life of a housewife is hard; there are hundreds of things to annoy her. But what other job can she get, on which she can sass her employer?

Deprived

Small boy at piano to mother:

"Gee, Mommy, I wish you hadn't been deprived of so many things as a child."

A Woman's Way

When a woman wants to celebrate or when she has the blues, she raids the family budget and buys a pair of shoes! And when she's really angry at something hubby'd done—she buys a very silly hat and wears it—just for fun!

No Liar

He had been fishing, but with poor luck. On his way home, he entered a fish market and said to the proprietor, "Pete, stand over there and throw me five of the biggest of those trout!"

"Throw 'em? What for?" asked the dealer in amazement.

"I want to tell my wife I caught them. I may be a poor fisherman, but I'm no liar."

Can't Understand

A small boy, being sent to bed by his mother, who had thoroughly fazzled nerves, was heard to say to his brother, "I can't figure it out. Every time she gets tired we have to take a nap."

Ignorance

There is one thing to be said in favor of ignorance—it surely causes a lot of interesting arguments.

How's That?

Two notices in the church bulletin of a Plymouth, England, church recently left the members in a quandary. One item read, "Strong drink is your worst enemy." Another one said, "Make your worst enemy your best friend."

How Would You Feel

An American astronaut was poised in his capsule, ready to be launched. "How do you feel?" he was asked.

"How would you feel," he replied, "if you were sitting here atop 150,000 parts—each supplied by the lowest bidder?"

Limited

"When I go to bed at night, I always see yellow lights and green dots before my eyes."

"Have you ever seen a psychiatrist?"

"No, only yellow lights and green dots."

A Gentleman

"My good man," said the customer to the grocery store owner, "how is it you have not called on me for my account?"

"Oh, I never ask a gentleman for money."

"Indeed! But what do you do if he doesn't pay?"

"Oh, after a certain time," said the owner, "I conclude he is not a gentleman, and then I ask him."

Credit

A father and son were closely examining a billiard table when the deparment store clerk sidled up.

"You only pay a small deposit," he said, "and then make no more payments for six months."

"Oh," the little boy said, "who told you about us?"

He Wins

At a little party of young folks there were just enough cookies for each to have three. But little Bobby took four.

"You're supposed to get only three cookies, Bobby," said the hostess. "You ought to put the fourth one back."

"Can't," exclaimed Bobby, "I ate that one first."

Candor

One has to admire the candor of the politician in a Tennessee city who announced his candidacy for reelection in these words: "My many friends have not prevailed upon me to become a candidate for reelection, and I have not been told that the city needs my services. The truth of the matter is simply this: I want the job again."

Revenge

A plumber received a desperate midnight call from a doctor. "Hate to call you at this hour," he said, "but I have a plumbing emergency—a bathroom pipe is leaking badly. Hurry over."

"Tell you what to do," said the plumber. "Take two aspirins every four hours, drop them down the pipe. If the leak doesn't stop by morning, phone me at the office."

Two Burdens

Grandma, advising young bride: "I hope your lot will be easier than mine. I've had two burdens—Pa and the fire. Every time I turn to look at one, the other goes out."

Difficult to Draw

The third graders were asked to draw pictures of what they wanted to be when they grew up. One little boy turned in a picture of himself as an airplane pilot. Another drew himself driving a fire engine. But one little girl turned in a blank piece of paper.

When the teacher asked why, she explained, "I want to be married—but I don't know how to draw it."

Hazard

A friend gave a woman a young alligator three feet long. Not knowing what to do with it she put it in the bathtub. She went out shopping and when she returned to her apartment she found this note from her maid who had come in during her absence.

"Dear Madam: Sorry to have to resign. I refuse to work in a house where there is an alligator in the bathtub. I would have told you this before, but I did not think the matter would ever come up."

Difficult

Two elderly ladies were sitting by the window one Sunday evening. One of them, listening to the church choir across the street, exclaimed, "How beautifully they sing!"

The other, listening to the crickets on the front lawn, replied. "Yes, and I've been told they do it with their hind legs."

Return the Compliment

Today's children insist that their elders treat them as grown-ups; which wouldn't be bad if only the kids would return the compliment.

Plenty of Space

"You haven't many buildings in this new town of yours."

"I know," responded the enthusiastic subdivision promoter, "but look at the parking space."

Silence

A tourist spending the night in a small Vermont town joined a group of men sitting on the porch of the general store. After several vain attempts to start a conversation, he finally asked, "Is there a law against talking in this town?"

"No law against it," answered one Vermonter, "but there's an understanding that no one speaks unless he's sure he can improve on silence."

Seldom at Least

The teacher was quizzing her pupils on natural history.

"Now, Bobby," she asked, "tell me where the elephant is found."

Bobby struggled for the answer. Finally his face lighted up and he replied: "The elephant is so big that he is never lost."

She Started It

Slippery ice, very thin; pretty girl tumbled in. Saw a boy upon the bank—gave a shriek, and then she sank. Boy on bank heard her shout, jumped right in—helped her out. Now he's hers—very nice; but she had to break the ice.

Diplomacy

A diplomat is a gentleman who can tell a lie in such a manner to another gentleman (who is also a diplomat) that the second gentleman is compelled to let on that he really believes the first gentleman, although he knows that the first gentleman is a liar, who knows that the second gentleman does not believe him, yet both let on that each believes the other, while both know that both are liars.

Freedom of Speech

An American and a Russian soldier faced one another across the barriers of East and West Berlin. In time they fell into an argument.

"In my country," said the American, "I can go to the door of the White House, ring the bell, and say just what I think of our President."

"So what?" said the Russian contemptuously. "In my country I can go to the gate of the Kremlin and say just what I think about your President."

Southern Hospitality

The late James Thurber liked to tell the story about two Alaskans who spent a summer vacation in the northernmost tip of Maine and had the time of their lives. As they left, one of them told their hosts effusively: "Thank you so much. Now I know what they mean by southern hospitality."

Television

Television enables people with nothing to say to talk to people who aren't listening.

Foreign to Him

A Navajo Indian was asked whether he spoke any foreign language.

"Yes," he replied, "English."

Thank Goodness

Little Tommy: "Mommy, teacher asked me if I have any brothers and sisters who will be coming to school."

Mother: "That's nice of her to take an interest in us. What did she say when you told her you are an only child?"

Tommy: "All she said was, 'Thank goodness.' "

Better Idea

A man once told Mark Twain: "Before I die I intend to make a pilgrimage to the Holy Land, climb Mount Sinai, and read the Ten Commandments."

"I have a better idea," said Twain. "Stay right at home in Boston and keep them."

To the Head of the Class

"What color would you paint the sun and wind in a picture, George?" asked the art teacher.

"I would paint the sun rose and the wind blue," answered quick-witted George.

That's the Trouble

Three men were talking one day about the frailties of people. Said one man, "The trouble with most people is that they eat too much."

The second man objected, and said, "It isn't how much you eat, but what you eat that counts."

The third man, a doctor, said, "It's neither what you eat or how much. It's what's eating you that is important."

She Is Absent

Eight-year-old Susie was crazy about school, while her six-year-old sister was less enthusiastic.

"Let's play school," suggested Susie one day.

"All right," agreed the younger one grudgingly, "but let's play I'm absent today."

He Can't Remember

"We spent our vacation in the car touring the entire country."

"Touring, eh? You must have passed through some beautiful country."

"Oh, we must have! After all, we averaged over 500 miles a day on the trip."

Everyone Move Up

The proud sixteen-year-old boy turned into the driveway at the wheel of the family car. Several younger brothers came running.

"I passed my driver's test!" shouted the teen-ager. "You guys can all move up one bike."

Short Summer

Alaskan (to newcomer): "We have very short summers here. Last year it was on a Tuesday."

He Wanted to Go Along

The time had come for the farm lad to start feeling his oats. He approached his father and said, "Dad, I'm leaving home. I'm going to find fame, adventure, fortune . . . Don't try to stop me, Dad, my mind's made up."

The old man jumped from his chair. "Who's trying to stop you!" he exclaimed. "I'm going with you, boy!"

Correct

The bright young boy was taking a test but seemed to be stumped on the question which read: "Give the number of tons of coal shipped out of the United States in any given year."

After a few minutes of thought, the boy wrote: "A.D. 32—none."

It Certainly Is

A personnel director, interviewing an applicant for a job, said, "You ask pretty high wages for a man with no experience."

"Well," the man said, "it's harder work when you don't know anything about it."

Simple Question

Two secretaries were discussing their troubles during their coffee break. "All I asked him," moaned one, "was if he wanted the carbon copy double spaced, too."

Experience Speaks

Several members of the faculty were discussing what most people wanted to get out of a new car.

"Dependability," said one fellow. "Styling," replied another. "Economy," stated the third.

Just then the principal entered the room, and the group decided to pose the question to him, inasmuch as he had recently purchased a new automobile. "What is the thing you'd most like to get out of your new car?" he was asked.

"My teen-age son!" he replied.

A Second Helping

Traveler: "I'm sorry, conductor. My dog has eaten my ticket."

Conductor: "Well, then, may I suggest you buy him a second helping?"

Soup

When Bobby Clark, sampling a bowl of soup was asked by the waiter, "How's the soup, sir?" he answered reflectively, "To tell you the truth, I'm kinda sorry I stirred it."

Medicine

With modern medicine doing so well at increasing life expectancy, we'd better be careful about adding to the national debt—we might have to pay it off ourselves instead of passing it on.

So Would I

Teacher: "How would you punctuate this sentence, 'I saw a five-dollar bill on the sidewalk?' "

Jimmy: "I wouldn't punctuate it at all. I'd make a dash after it."

A Young Scientist

The fact-finding youngster faced his mother one day, saying, "Didn't you tell me the stork brought me?"

"Why yes, dear."

"And I weighed eight pounds?"

"Yes."

"Well, for your information," said the boy, "a stork doesn't have the wingspread to carry an eight-pound load!"

Hello-Goodbye

"Well, well, Dad," said his son breezily. "How're things going at the grindstone? I just dropped into the office to say 'hello.' "

"That's fine, my boy," said the father, "but your mother and sister just dropped in to say 'hello' too, and they got all I had."

Looks

Customer: I don't like the looks of that trout.

Storekeeper: Well, if you want looks, why don't you buy a goldfish?

Be Careful, Judge

Congressman Blowhard: "Your Honor, I admit I may have been driving a bit fast, but I would like to point out that I am a congressman, and ..."

Judge: "Ignorance is no excuse."

Correct

Lawyer: Are you married?

Witness: Yah.

Lawyer: Whom did you marry?

Witness: I married a woman.

Lawyer: Do you know anyone who didn't?

Witness: Ya! My sister married a man.

Not Easy

Wishing to do the right thing, the motorist stopped his car and started back in search of the farmer whose rooster he had hit.

"Pardon me," said the motorist, "I killed your rooster with my car and I came to let you know I'm willing to replace him."

"Hmmmmmm," mused the farmer, "let's hear you crow."

Mistake

Friend: I think I saw your wife downtown today. She was trying to park between two trucks.

Husband: Did she make it?

Friend: Yes.

Husband: Then it wasn't my wife.

Income Tax

In fact many books have been written on humorous letters sent to the Internal Revenue Service. One that I have enjoyed was edited by Bill Adler last year with such letters as:

In reply to an inquiry from his Internal Revenue District, one puzzled citizen wrote back—"as far as I can determine, I never engaged any Internal Revenue Service. Will you kindly explain the transactions to which your recent form letter referred?"

"Sir: If these answers will not do, please schedule an inquest at your nearest local office."

A taxpayer who had several arguments over the years with his Internal Revenue Service wrote in after a lengthy lull:

"After many months of peaceful coexistence, I suppose we are both ready to resume our battle."

One district director received a reply from a taxpayer who had failed to file an information return. Scrawled across the form was the statement:

"I have been dead for almost a year."

Another one wrote:

"Sir: Tell the President, no more income tax cuts. I couldn't afford this one."—*Richard T. Cragg*

Be Careful

A sergeant was explaining some important points to a squad of recruits on the rifle range. "This type of bullet will penetrate two feet of wood," he said. "So remember to keep your heads down."

Smart Fellow

Sheriff: "Got away, did he? Did you guard all the exits?"

Policeman: "Yes, but we think he must have left by one of the entrances."

It Happens

The little woman had spent the whole afternoon, and made a real effort to balance up her checkbook. When her husband came home, she handed him four neatly-typed sheets, with items and costs in their respective columns. He read them over carefully: "Milkman, $11.25, cleaners, $4.75 etc." Everything was clear except one item reading "ESP, $24.89."

Warily he asked, "what does ESP mean?"

She smiled, "Error some place."

Can't Escape

Two Eskimos took a room in a summer hotel. To their surprise, they were attacked by mosquitoes, an insect new to them. That night, as they turned off the light and went to bed, two fireflies flitted in through the window.

"It's no use," one groaned to the other. "They've come back with lanterns looking for us!"

We Stayed There

"Have a good night?" the hostess asked sweetly of the house guest who had slept on a couch.

"Fair to good," he answered sleepily. "I got up from time to time and rested."

The No. 1 Problem

Little Edna seemed to be enjoying herself thoroughly at the zoo with her father. As they were looking at the lions, however, Edna began to look very troubled. Her father asked her the trouble.

"I was just wondering, Daddy," she replied in a fearful voice, "if a lion broke loose and ate you, what bus do I take home?"

Sounds Reasonable

A memorandum on a phone call was handed to a local businessman by his secretary. "I can't read this," he said.

"I couldn't understand him very well," said the secretary, "so I didn't write it very clearly."

Inflation

Something that cost $5 to buy a few years ago now costs $10 to repair.

Money

They say that money doesn't bring happiness, but it's nice to be able to find out for yourself.

In Days of Old

In days of old when knights were bold and barons held their sway, they took their orders from their wives just as men do today.

The Bills

I love to think of Christmas, the mistletoe and holly, the shopping crowds and drifted snow, and gifts—all seem so jolly. I love to think of Christmas, that time of joy and laughter, but what makes me weak is to think of the bills that follow after!

If

A fellow who had owed a bill several months, and ignored statements and pleas for a remittance, finally received a curt notice that the account would be placed with an attorney for collection unless paid at once. Thereupon the dilatory debtor took up his pen and wrote the creditor as follows: "Enclosed find check to settle the account referred to in your note of yesterday. Thanking you for being so patient with me, I remain, yours truly." Then below was a postscript: "This is the kind of letter I would write you if I had the money."

Confidential

A Russian was convicted by a Soviet court for calling the Minister of Culture a fool. He got 20 years: 5 years for slander and 15 years for revealing a state secret.

One Explanation

Teacher: "Now, see if you can understand what the word "sufficient" means. If I gave a cat a bowl of milk, that might not be sufficient. But if I gave a cat two bowls of milk, that would be sufficient. Now Jimmy, what does the word mean?"

Jimmy: "A cat full of milk."

Willie Was Right

Willie was none too bright, but he always had an answer. The teacher was drilling the class on the mysteries of mathematics. "Willie," she said, "how much is nine and six?"

"Thirteen," said Willie.

"No. Try again."

"Sixteen."

"No."

"Willie, Willie," said the teacher, "why couldn't you guess a smaller number—fifteen say?"

"Oh, no," said Willie, "it couldn't be fifteen."

"Why couldn't it?" asked the teacher.

"Because," said Willie, "ten and five make fifteen."

One Benefit?

A school teacher was trying to explain subtraction to his young pupils. "You have ten fingers," he said to one youngster. "Suppose you had three less, then what would you have?"

Came the prompt reply, "No music lessons."

Serious Matter

Bob Burns told one on an uncle of his who was a judge back in Van Buren. Court was in session. The courtroom was filled with noisy onlookers. After several cases had been handled, the judge rapped his gavel loudly and stormed out: "You folks are just simply gonna have to be a little quieter if you stay in this courtroom. I have had to convict the last five men without hearing a word of the testimony!"

Looking Ahead

We know the fellow who gave his wife a $1,000 check last year for Christmas. Attached was a note saying, "If business is good, I'll sign it."

It's Bad

For three nights father had struggled dutifully to help his little daughter unravel the puzzling arithmetic problems she had been given for homework. They were not making much progress.

"Daddy, it's going to be even worse next week," she warned.

"What happens next week?" he demanded, his drooping spirits sinking to his boots.

"Next week," she said, "we start learning the dismal system."

He Knew the Date

"How long have you worked for the company?"

"Ever since the boss threatened to fire me."

That's Different

When a very throaty tenor finished his song in a talent contest, there was only a smattering of applause, but one man in the audience kept repeating to himself in a voice scarcely audible to those nearby. "Extraordinary! Wonderful! Unbelievable!"

"Pardon me, sir," said a puzzled man sitting in the next seat to him. "I know a little something about music and take my word for it, that fellow cannot sing. I don't see how you can sit there and say his voice was extraordinary and wonderful!"

"Not his voice," explained the first man, "but his nerve—his colossal nerve."

One Explanation

Mary Jane, aged six, was looking at photographs of her parents' wedding. Her father described the ceremony and tried to explain its meaning. Suddenly the light dawned.

"Oh," Mary Jane exclaimed. "Is that when you got Mother to come to work for us?"

Telephone

Calling my wife on the telephone is a task that makes me dizzy. When the wire is clear, she isn't home, and when she's home, it's busy.

Pretty Bad

An Arab furtively stepped on a scale near the end of a lingering day; a counterfeit coin he dropped in the slot and silently stole a weigh.

Take Your Choice

A poll taken to determine the most popular salutations exchanged between husbands and wives listed these winners, in order: Dear, Darling, Baby, Honey, Sweetheart, Dearest, Precious.

Come, Come

Diner (sarcastically to second diner who is smoking a cigar at the same table):

"I hope you don't mind my eating while you smoke."

Second diner: "Not at all, provided I can still hear the orchestra."

Sounds Logical

A visitor was walking through the village and the church bells were ringing. He saw an old man and said to him: "Why are the bells ringing?"

"Because the parson is pulling the ropes," he replied.

Extra Reward

A quickie movie producer, short of cash, was trying to persuade one hungry actor to appear in his picture for an incredibly small fee.

"I know it's not much," the producer apologized, "but I'm sure you'll be glad you took the part."

"For that miserable fee?" the actor scoffed.

"Not just for the fee," the producer explained, "in the first and last scenes you eat a sandwich."

Long Wait

A small boy in a department store was standing near the escalator watching the moving handrail.

"Something wrong, son?" inquired a floorwalker.

"Nope," replied the boy. "Just waiting for my chewing gum to come back.

Certainly

The man had barely paid off his mortgage on the house when he mortgaged it again to buy a car, and not too long after borrowed money to build a garage. His banker hesitated, and said, "If I do make this new loan, how will you buy gas for the car?"

"It seems to me," the man replied curtly, "that a fellow who owns a big house, a car, and garage, should be able to get credit for gas."

Conference

A meeting at which people talk about what they should be doing.

Winter

We may complain about the heat in the summer, but at least we don't have to shovel it.

Chemistry

One of the first things a boy learns with a chemistry set is that he isn't likely to get another one.

He Had a Problem

He could not have been more than five, and he was a pathetic little figure as he carried his suitcase down the front steps of his home. Around the block he trudged, and around again. In fact, he kept walking around the block until it got dark and a policeman stopped him.

"What's the idea?" the officer asked the youngster.

"Running away," explained the lad sadly.

"Look, I've had my eye on you," said the officer, "and you've been doing nothing but walking around the block. Do you call that running away, sonny?"

"Well, what do you want me to do?" cried the boy, tearfully. "I'm not allowed to cross the street alone."

We've Had It Happen

"I beg your pardon," said the man returning to his seat in the theater, "but did I step on your toes when I left?"

"You sure did," came the reply.

"Good, I am in the right row."

It Isn't Easy

A tired-looking man dragged himself through his front door and slumped into a chair.

"Busy day at the office, dear?" his wife asked sympathetically.

"Terrible," he sighed. "The computer broke down in the middle of the afternoon and we all had to think."

That's Different

The boss called the new stenographer into his office. "Miss Hawkins," he said, "you're the best-looking girl we've had working in this office. You dress well, you have a nice voice, you make a good impression on the public, and your manners are excellent."

"Oh, thank you," she said, "your compliments are very pleasing."

"Enjoy them to the fullest," added the boss, "because now we are going to discuss your spelling, punctuation, and typing."

Don't Worry

An old lady went to the post office to mail a package and, fearing she didn't use enough stamps, she asked the clerk to weigh it.

After weighing it the clerk told her she'd actually used too many. "Oh, dear," she said, "I do hope it won't go too far."

Hard Luck

Uncle: "Hello, my boy. You're not looking very happy. What's the matter?"

Small nephew: "Aunt Sally said I could eat as many cookies as I wanted—and I can't."

Even As You and I

A fool there was who had worked like heck, even as you and I.

He saved his dough till he had a peck, then he bought an auto and made a wreck of his hard-earned dough of which he had a peck, and now he is in debt clear up to his neck, even as you and I.

Being Merry

It is easy enough to be merry when there isn't a jolt or a jar, but the man worthwhile is the man who can smile when his wife is driving the car.

If

I'd be the Captain of my Soul when Life's grim storm clouds thicken. I'd be the Master of my Fate—if I were not so chicken!

He Knew His Rights

A Kentucky first grader recently proved how practical school children can really be. He slipped in the hall of his school and skinned his knee. A teacher proffered psychological first aid with, "Remember, big boys don't cry." The boy replied, "I'm not gonna cry, I'm gonna sue."

Naturally

A young mother took every precaution to insure a sanitary surrounding for her infant son. Up to the time he was four months old visitors were required to wear face masks. One day the mother said to the father:

"Alexander seems to be cutting a tooth, and I suppose I should find out about it somehow."

"Well," suggested the husband, "my mother used to put her finger in the baby's mouth and . . . "

Noticing the horrified look on his wife's face, he quickly added: "Of course, you boil the finger first."

They Probably Haven't Heard Any

There is one nice thing about babies. They don't go around bragging about the bright things their fathers and mothers have said.

Bargain Rates At Special Times

Housewife: "How much are pork chops?"

Butcher: "Fifty cents a pound."

Housewife: "The butcher across the street sells them for forty cents a pound."

Butcher: "Why don't you buy them from him?"

Housewife: "He hasn't any today."

Butcher: "Oh. Well, when I don't have any, I sell them for twenty cents a pound."

Good Idea

High school principal, speaking to a group of businessmen: "We require our boys to take English class for four years. We believe they should learn to speak a language other than their own."

Fits Real Good

A certain husband was angry because his wife had bought a very expensive fur coat. "Why did you have to spend so much money?" he roared.

"Well, dear," confessed his contrite wife, "I guess Satan tempted me too much."

"Then why didn't you say, 'Get thee behind me, Satan'?"

"Darling, I did, but he just looked over my shoulder and said, 'Fits you real good in the back, too, dearie.'"

No Good

A modern mother and her young son were shopping in a supermarket. The child, trying to help, picked up a package and brought it to her. "No, no, honey," protested the mother, "go put it back. You have to cook that."

Her Own Dark

Mother, to small daughter who wanted the light left on: "But you sleep in the dark at home, dear. Why not here at Grandma's?"

Daughter: "Yes, but it's my own dark at home, Mommy."

That's Good

"John," she said, "I've got a lot of things I want to talk to you about tonight."

"Good," replied John. "Usually you want to talk about a lot of things you haven't got."

It's Easy

A golf pro, employed by a club to give lessons, was approached by two smarties. "Do you wish to learn to play golf?" the pro asked them.

"Not me," said one, "It's Bill here. He wants to learn. I learned yesterday."

Diet

Doctor, to portly patient: "Follow this diet and in a couple of months I want to see three fourths of you back here for a checkup."

Not So Fast

A stranger sauntered up the sidewalk before a modest, new ranch house in a small midwestern city. "Nice house you got here," he observed to the owner. "Worth about $20,000, I imagine."

"Nope," retorted the owner, "it's worth every cent of $33,000. Are you looking for a place to buy?"

"No," replied the stranger, jotting something in a notebook, "I'm just the new tax assessor."

Different

The Sunday School teacher was describing how Lot's wife looked back and turned into a pillar of salt.

Little Johnny was much interested. "My mother looked back once, while she was driving," he explained, "and she turned into a telephone pole!"

No Ordinary People

Overheard on the fringe of Gramercy Park, smartly costumed mother to teen-age daughter: "You must understand, dear, that we're not the sort of people who give clever names to cats."—*New Yorker*

Scared

My wife was in a minor auto bump, but she did sustain a cracked rib or two. She hadn't been to church for some time, so she appeared the following Sunday. After the service the minister was shaking hands at the front door with members of the congregation when he saw her coming down the aisle. His face wrinkled into a broad grin and he said: "Scared you, didn't it?"—*George T. Armitage*

They Won

A college swimming coach was summarizing his team's achievements at the annual athletic banquet. "Well, we didn't win any meets," he conceded, "but we all had a good time, and nobody drowned."

Crime

A very good idea for making sure that crime doesn't pay would be to let the government run it.

It Often Does

An African chief who returned from his first visit to Europe gave this report to his people: "Thousands of people assembled in seats around a great green field. Two groups of men in odd dress ran onto the field, made bending motions and placed themselves in special positions. Then the chief man kicked an object bigger than any egg, and the miracle was produced: Rains fell from the heavens."

Real Fun

The father of a ten-year-old boy looked at his pride and joy watching television with a bored expression, then remarked, "When I was your age, son, I walked miles in blizzards, milked four cows early each morning, and rode a horse instead of riding in a comfortable car. What do you think of that?"

The boy looked up at his father and remarked, "I wish we could have that kind of fun now."

Social Security

When a boy has the only football or baseball in the neighborhood.

Three Kinds

There are three kinds of people: The few who make things happen; the many who watch things happen, and those who have no idea what has happened.

Questions

For asking questions Bobby has a flair. His weary parents call him their little question heir!

Yet, It'll

You try to write—no ink will trickle. Put pen in pocket, and instantly it'll.

A Brave Boy

A couple of young boys walked into a dentist's office. One faced him boldly and said: "I want a tooth out and I don't want no gas 'cause I'm in a hurry."

"I must say you're a brave boy," said the dentist. "Which tooth is it?"

The little boy turned to his silent friend and said: "Show him your tooth, Albert."

Certainly, It's Free

The alert filling-station attendant had checked the oil and gas and was cleaning the windshield when the woman driver asked: "And would you mind going over Johnny's face just once?"

Courageous

An admirer came up to a senatorial candidate after his speech and said: "Congratulations. That was a fine speech. I like the straightforward way you dodged those issues."

Unconstitutional

A customer complained that the new barber was driving him crazy with his incessant chatter.

The proprietor observed mildly, "According to the Constitution of the United States, he's got a right to talk."

"That may be," admitted the customer, "but the United States has a Constitution that can stand it. Mine can't."

He Wasn't So Dumb

A psychiatrist was making one of his visits to a mental institution. He was particularly intrigued by one patient who sat huddled in a corner scratching himself for hours at a time. The doctor finally approached the unfortunate and asked quietly: "Would you like to tell me why you sit here all day scratching yourself?"

"Because," replied the man, heaving a great sigh, "I'm the only one in the whole world who knows where I itch."

No Spendthrift

A traffic policeman found the following remarks on a piece of paper fastened to an obviously defective parking meter: "I put three nickels in the meter.—10-462" (license).

"So did I.—76-495."

"I'm not going to pay a nickel to find out if these guys are lying.—87-965."

Diet

The second day of a diet is always easier than the first. By the second day you're off it.—*Jackie Gleason*

Lazy

It takes a mighty conscientious man to tell whether he's tired or just lazy.

Definitions

"Obstetrician: A doctor who makes money on the stork market ... Road map: A piece of paper that helps you get lost ... Detour: A route on which you can't find anyone to ask where you are . . . National Hobby: Coin collecting . . . Middle age: When your spring fancy lightly turns to liver pills . . . Income taxes: The first robbin' of spring."

Fear

We have always enjoyed the story of the man who went with his wife to the mountains for a vacation trip. One day he returned to their cabin from a hike all scratched and bruised and told her that he had met a snake on the trail. She said, "But don't you remember the guide told us yesterday that the snakes up here are not poisonous?" He replied, "They don't have to be when they can make you jump off a fifty-foot cliff."—*Arkansas Methodist*

Same Department

The parson paying calls in his parish knocked at the door of a family in his congregation. A woman's voice called out, "Is that you, Angel?"

"No," came the minister's prompt reply, "but I'm from the same department."

Appearance First

The sweet young thing was asked which of the following traits she desired in a husband: brains, money or appearance.

"Appearance," snapped the girl, "And the sooner the better."

Advertising

In warning-size letters on the rear end of a very large transport truck appears the ad of an enterprising automobile repair man:

If I stop before you do
Take your smashed radiator to
John Brown
Auto Repairman

Stay in the Shuffle

It is reported that a firm in Denver received the following letter from a client whom they had pressed for a settlement:

"Once a month we put all our outstanding accounts on the table, draw six at random, and pay them. If we receive any more of your impudent letters, you won't even get a place in the shuffle next month."

Insecure

Mother of a small boy to child psychiatrist: "Well, I don't know whether or not he feels insecure, but everybody else in the neighborhood certainly does!"—*Gerber News*

Good Reason

She made a right-hand turn from a left-hand lane and promptly hit another auto. The driver got out and accosted her: "Lady, why didn't you signal?"

"Because I always turn here."

We Can Understand

A stout middle-aged suburbanite was explaining his tennis technique.

"My brain barks a command to my body. It says: 'Run forward speedily. Slam the ball over the net. Then run back and get into position for the next shot.' "

"Then what happens?" he was asked.

"Then," he replied, "my body says: 'Who me?' "

Looking Ahead

A proud grandmother was out for a stroll with two visiting grandsons when she met up with an old friend.

"My, what handsome boys!" exclaimed the friend. "How old are they?"

"The doctor," said the grandmother, "is four and the railroad engineer is three."

Trouble in Writing

A college grid coach had just lost his outstanding freshman prospect, by way of academic dismissal.

"It's going to be quite a loss to the team," commented a sympathetic sportswriter.

"It sure is," wailed the coach. "Why, that boy could do everything with a football—except autograph it!"

Marry

By all means marry. If you get a good wife, you become very happy; if you get a bad one, you will become a philosopher —and that is good for every man.—*Socrates*

Dead End

After Calvin Coolidge made it known that he did not choose to run again for the Presidency, he was besieged by reporters for a more elaborate statement. One member of the press was more persistent than the others, and asked him, "Exactly why don't you want to run for President again, Mr. Coolidge?"

The President's solemn reply: "No chance for advancement."

An Example

An elderly citizen went to his doctor and said, "Doctor, I need your help about my memory. I am having a great deal of difficulty with it."

"Give us an example of your difficulty," asked the doctor.

"Why, what difficulty are you referring to?"

Simple

An economist spoke on the "whys" and "wherefores" of our economic system. He spoke for an hour and covered the subject well. Following him, the chairman said:

Ladies and gentlemen, what our speaker has been telling you is that, if your outgo exceeds your income, your upkeep will be your downfall."

Second Thought

A lady declared the other day that second thoughts were best. Then she continued, "Man was God's first thought; woman was His second."

Las Vegas

Radar studies indicate that Venus is a hot, waterless desert. To make it really popular with tourists they will have to add legalized gambling.

New York City

A tourist in New York eagerly opened his fortune cookie at a chop suey center. It read "Never mind your hat and coat. They're towing your car away outside."—*Jim Backus*

For A Moment

Photographer: "Look pleasant, please. As soon as I snap this picture you can resume your natural expression."

Confusion

Four women with one luncheon check.

Try, Try, Again

An amateur carpenter sawed off a board three times and it was still too short.

Taxes

A state we are deep in the heart of.

Enjoyment

I always enjoy myself. It's the other people I have trouble enjoying.—*Groucho Marx*

Ego

Once upon a time there was an actor without any ego. And he ended up getting conceited about that.—*Ade Kahn*

Next

A young boy of 5 was fishing in a bucket in his front yard when a passerby stopped and asked, with a twinkle in his eye: "How many have you caught, young fellow?"

"You're the third," the boy replied.

A Confession

A confession by the ever-ailing Oscar Levant: "I've tried everything to get well. I've even laughed. And you know how I hate having a good time."

Hard Advice

"You are very run down," said the doctor to his patient. "I suggest you lay off golf for a while and get a good day in now and then at the office."

A Mop

A father, angry at his daughter because of her hairdo, stormed, "You girls of today don't mind if your hair looks like a mop." To which the daughter replied, "What is a mop?"

Martini Miracle

Did you ever try to explain to your son why a bottle of pop will spoil his dinner . . . while a martini perks up your appetite?

Cornered

Young married couples start out with wall-to-wall carpeting and back-to-the-wall financing.—*The Dearborn (Mich.) Press*

Absentee

The adult world is perplexing to moppets.

Three-year-old Barry Briggs adamantly refused to leave his pennies at Sunday school, despite his mother's instructions.

The fourth Sunday he trotted home with them his mother reiterated, "That money is for Jesus. Don't you want to give it to Him?"

"He never comes," explained Barry.—*Westby Times*

Definitions

Street cleaner: Rubble rouser.

Back-fence gossiping: A good way to gas the time.

Crowded igloo: The cold folks at home.

Football: A game in which the players run and the spectators kick.

Podiatrist: A person who listens to your wail of toe.

Repartee: What you think of 24 hours too late.

Rush Hour: When traffic moves at a snail's pace.

Theory and Practice: Theory is what is hard to understand and practice is what is hard to explain.

Middle Age: When you look forward to a dull evening.

Alarm Clock: A mechanism used to scare the daylights into you.

Committee: A body of people that keeps minutes and loses hours.

War: One thing you can't get in an economy size.

Scalp Massage: Pats on the belfry.

Hygiene: Taking a bath when you haven't been playing baseball.—*Sam Levenson*

Psychiatrist: One who lives off the fret of the land.

Castor Oil: Uhg Nog.

Sewing Circle: A group of knit wits.

Cocktail Party: Where you spear olives and stab friends.

The Jones Family
Every time I catch up with my neighbors, they refinance.

That's Different
A doctor called a plumber to repair a faucet washer, which the plumber easily replaced in five minutes. When the doctor saw the $7 bill, he remarked:

"Do you realize that I only get $6 for house calls?"

"Ah, yes," replied the plumber, "but I guarantee my work."

Nurse
The night nurse in the hospital is the one who wakes you up to ask if the day nurse gave you your sleeping pill.

She Knew the Answer
Two girls were talking about their plans. One said she intended to get a job as an airline stewardess. "That way," she said, "I'll meet lots of men."

"Might be an idea," agreed her companion, "but wouldn't you meet as many men doing something else?"

The first girl shrugged and said: "Maybe, but not strapped down."

Simple

Two hunters had been in the woods for several hours and one of them had been growing uneasy. Finally panic overcame him.

"We're lost!" he cried. "What are we going to do?"

"Take it easy," said his friend. "Shoot an extra deer and the game warden will be here in a minute and a half."

Don't Be Certain, Doctor

The old Scotsman lay dying and his wife and doctor stood by. The good man closed his eyes and the doctor, feeling the patient's pulse, said, "I'm afraid he's gone." Weakly the man opened his eyes and murmured, "Not quite yet, Doctor."

"Hold your tongue, mon," said his wife. "How should you be knowing better than our doctor?"

The Expert

The handyman who did everything well is now replaced by the expert who does one thing poorly, more expensively, and at his own dilatory convenience.

Hit a Triple

The little fellow put all his 60 pounds into a ferocious swing and connected—barely. The ball jiggled straight back to the pitcher, who fumbled it a moment. There was plenty of time to nail the batter at first, but the pitcher's throw soared high over the first baseman's head. The slugger flew on toward second. Somebody retrieved the ball. The next throw sailed into left field. The hitter swaggered into third, puffing through a man-sized grin. "Oh, boy!" he said. "That's the first triple I ever hit in my whole life."

Advertising

The manager of a department store put this notice in the window: "If you need it, we have it."

But in the window of a rival, a sign appeared stating, "If we don't have it, you don't need it."

Carry It Fast

As the explorer explained to the visitor, wild animals will not harm you if you carry a torch—especially if you carry it fast enough.

Looked Healthy

Kanu had just taken a photograph of an old man on his 98th birthday. He thanked the old man saying, "I hope to be around to take your picture when you're 100."

The old man replied, "Why not? You look pretty healthy."

Still Rhymes

Teacher, commenting on little boy's poem: "Since your poem is about flowers, Wilbur, I think the word 'smell' would be more appropriate. You can still have it rhyme by substituting the word 'blue-bell' for 'mountain pink.' "

Has Done Enough

Archie, age 12, was puzzled over his social problems and discussed them with his friend, Mortimer.

"I have walked to school with this girl three times," he said, "and I've carried her books, and I bought her ice cream twice. Now do you think I oughta kiss her?"

"Naw," said Mortimer. "You've done enough for her already."

Not Too Bad

"I've learned a lot about the new neighbors today," the little woman told her husband. "They have no car, no television no piano. I can't imagine what they do have!"

From behind his paper, her spouse suggested mildly, "A bank account, perhaps!"

Getting Discouraged

"You told me how good you were when I hired you two weeks ago," said a foreman to one of his men. "Now tell me all over again, I'm gettting discouraged."

Pretty Tricky

The neighborhood borrower approached Mr. Smith Saturday noon and inquired, "Say, Smith, are you using your lawnmower today—this afternoon?"

"Why, yes, I intended to cut the grass this afternoon," replied Smith warily.

"Fine," exclaimed the borrower. "Then you won't be needing your golf clubs. I'll just borrow them."

Suitable Today

"This looks too complicated for a young child," the mother said to the salesman in the toy department.

"It's an educational toy designed to adjust a child to live in the world today," explained the clerk. "Any way he puts it together . . . it's wrong."

What's Funny?

Hermione Gingold on comedy: It's jolly well difficult to make people laugh these days. By the time they've arrived at the theater, paid for two tickets, and shelled out for a baby sitter, I mean, what have they got to laugh at?

Odd

Senator Dirksen, in announcing he was making a second recording, mentioned that the performers' union had been after him to join. "It does seem a little odd, doesn't it," he said, "that I would have to join local 1089 to give my interpretation of the Lord's Prayer."

The End of the Month

Scientists tell us that we're taller in the morning than we are in the evening. Most of us have noticed, too, that we're shorter around the end of the month.

Home

The number of accidents in the home is rising; people aren't spending enough time there to know their way around.

Snowed Under

We're doing twice as much clerical work as we used to do. We don't know any more than we did, but now we're putting it on paper.

Easier

Getting to the moon looks easier and easier as time passes. It's staying right here on earth that seems tougher and tougher.

All O.K.

A man telephoned the police to report that thieves had been at work on his car. "They've stolen the steering wheel, the accelerator, the clutch pedal and the dashboard," he complained.

The police sergeant said he would investigate and hung up. Then the telephone rang again.

"Don't bother," said the same voice, this time with a hiccup. "I got into the back seat by mistake."

Biblical Students

A harried young salesman left his car in a no-parking zone with this note under the windshield wiper. "I have circled this block 20 times; if I don't keep this appointment, I'll lose my job. Forgive us our trespasses."

Finished with business, he returned to his car and found a ticket and this note: "I have circled this block for 20 years. If I don't give you a ticket, I'll lose my job. Lead us not into temptation."

I'll Slow Down

Small daughter: "Daddy, don't drive so fast."

"Why not?"

"Because the policeman on the motorcycle can't get by."

A Generation Ago

A generation ago most men who finished a day's work needed rest; now they need exercise.

Right Place

Sign in Optometrist's window: "If you don't see what you want, you've come to the right place."

He Had It

Employer: "Look here, what did you mean by telling me you had five years' experience when you've never had a job before?"

Young man: "Well, you advertised for a man with imagination."

Conversation

Speaking of his wife, the Weather Forecaster said: "She speaks about 150 words per minute, with gusts up to 190!"

Alumni

Every time you go to a class reunion you find your classmates are so stout and bald they hardly recognize you.

Getting Even

A woman who had been bitten by a dog was advised by her physician to write her last wishes, since she might soon succumb to hydrophobia. She spent so much time with pencil and paper that the doctor finally asked if it wasn't getting to be a pretty lengthy will.

"Will!" she snorted. "Nothing of the kind. I'm writing a list of people I'm going to bite."

It Happens to Every Husband

On the first day of Springtime my true love gives to me— five packs of seed, four sacks of fertilizer, three cans of weed killer, two bottles of insect spray, and a pruning knife for the pear tree.

Golf

If you watch a game, it's fun. If you play, it's recreation. If you work at it, it's golf.—*Bob Hope*

Ticket to the Moon, Please

An Indian told his son: "Some day this country will be ours again. White men will all go to the moon."

Easier

It is easier to let it go in one ear and out the other if you have a minimum in between.

It Works

Woman to bridge club members: "I have the most wonderful recipe for goulash—all I have to do is mention it to my husband and he says, 'Let's eat out.'"

Playing Safe

The little boy approached his father who was standing on the edge of a cliff, admiring the scenery. He piped, "Mama says it isn't safe here and you're either to come away or else give me the picnic basket."

He Couldn't Help It

"Richie," screamed his mother, "did you fall down with your new pants on?"

"Yes, Mom," replied Richie, "there wasn't time to take them off."

The Stork

Their aunt was escorting the two small girls around the zoo. While they were looking at the stork, she told them the legend of the bird and how it brought them to their mother.

The children looked at each other and one whispered, "Don't you think we ought to tell her the truth?"

A Record

A young woman was dialing a record store. Her dial finger slipped a notch and she got a wrong number. A man answered, and she asked, "Do you have 'Eyes of Blue' and 'Heart That's True?'"

"No," said the man, "but I've got a wife and nine children, including four sets of twins."

"Is that a record?" gasped the astonished young lady.

"Well, ma'am," was the answer, "We're not sure, but we think it is."

Pretty Bad Story

Did you hear about the two cannibals? One was cutting out pictures of people and eating them. Whereupon the other one asked: "Is that dehydrated stuff any good?"

Good Horse

Hunter: "Is your new hunting horse well-behaved?"

Friend: "He certainly is! Every time we come to a fence, he lets me go over first."

Happy Ending

Young Jonathan had been promised a new puppy for his 10th birthday, but had a hard time choosing between a dozen likely candidates at the pet shop. Finally he decided upon one nondescript shaggy puppy who was wagging his tail furiously.

Explained Jonathan, "I want the one with the happy ending."

It That Clear?

A little girl was describing her first experience in an elevator. "We got into a little room," she said, "and the upstairs came down."

The Party Was Good

Jimmy had been to a birthday party the day before, and his friend was regarding him enviously.

"How was the party?" he asked. "Did you have a good time?"

"Did I?" was the emphatic answer. "I'm not hungry yet!"

Not Any More

The youngster had been saving up enough money to buy her father a birthday gift. She was concerned about one thing, though. "I can't be running uptown every month to make payments," she complained to her mother. "Isn't there a store where they'll let you pay the whole thing at once?"

Is That Clear?

Jud was winding his pocket watch at the gate of his farmhouse when a traveling salesman drove up and asked: "What time is it, mister?"

"We don't give the time to strangers," answered Jud. "It's bad policy."

"How's that?" asked the salesman.

"Well, if I give you the time," explained Jud, "you'll want to thank me and then I'll want to know your name and you'll want to know mine. Then we'll sit down and have a friendly chat and eventually I'll invite you for supper. You'll meet my daughter who's pretty; and you'll want to date her, and she'll date you 'cause there ain't many men around here. Then you'll likely propose matrimony. She'll say, 'Go ask Pa's consent,' and you'll come to me, and I'll have to turn you down 'cause I don't want my daughter marryin' no salesman that ain't got a watch!"

Hard to Believe

Two nurses were folding diapers in the maternity ward. One observed, "I just can't believe that they're only 30% water."

He Was

Doctor: "Here's my bill for services. You can pay $100 down and $25 a week for the next fifteen weeks."

Patient: "Sounds like buying an automobile!"

Doctor: "I am."

Too Short a Time

During a court inquiry into an elevator accident case, a blonde was put on the stand. The insurance company's lawyer found many inconsistencies in her testimony and began to lose patience. "I suppose when the elevator began to fall, all your sins flashed before you?" he asked sarcastically.

"Oh, no," she answered. "We only dropped eight stories."

That's Different

"I know a fellow who can run a hundred yards in six seconds."

"Impossible! The world's record is nine and two tenths seconds."

"This fellow knows a short cut."

Innocent

The patrolman chased a careening car until it stopped against a telephone pole. Two inebriated men tumbled out, unhurt, still trying to sing.

"Who was driving?" demanded the officer.

The song died out, but neither answered.

"Were you driving?" the cop asked one of the men.

"Nope," came the answer. "I was in the back seat."

"Then you were driving," the policeman told the other.

"Nope," said the second man happily. "I was in the back seat too."

Attention Hunters

Suggestion to amateur deer hunters: If it doesn't wear a vest, a necktie, a mustache or a hat, and doesn't smoke a pipe, it's probably a cow.

Of Course

"I want to be procrastinated at the next corner," said the passenger to the bus driver.

"You want to be what?" demanded the driver.

"Read your dictionary, young man," said the high-brow passenger, "and you will find procrastination means 'put off.'"

That's What Happens

Salesman: "This model has a top speed of 130 miles an hour, and she'll stop on a dime."

Prospect: "What happens then?"

Salesman: "A little putty knife comes out and scrapes you off the windshield."

New System

A salesman was trying to sell a young wife an egg timer, "Your husband's eggs will be just right if you use this," he assured her.

"But I don't need it," she answered brightly. "Jack likes his eggs the way I do them. I just look through the window at the traffic lights, and give them three reds and two greens."

It Depends On Which Way

Teacher: "How much is one half of eight, Billie?"

Billie: "Which way shall I divide it?"

Teacher: "What do you mean, which way?"

Billie: "Well, crosswise, one half would be 0, and lengthwise, 3."

He Knew

Teacher: "If you mowed twenty lawns at a dollar and a half each, what would you have?"

Tommy: "A new bicycle."

128

No Time for This Joke

The question was asked the other day that if a man smashed a clock, should he be convicted of killing time? Our opinion would be no, if the clock struck first.

Good Question

Father: "The trouble with you, son, is that you are always wishing for things you haven't got."

Son: "I know, Dad, but what else would I wish for?"

No Deal

A clergyman advertised for a man servant. The following day a young man called on him.

"Well," asked the clergyman, "can you light the fire and bring early morning tea at seven?"

"I — I think I could," replied the young man, puzzled.

"Can you work in the garden?" continued the clergyman. "I mean, can you mow the lawn and prune trees and cultivate the soil?"

"Well — er —yes, I think so," stammered the youth.

"Can you polish silver, look after a dog, and be generally useful about the house?"

The young man nodded.

"And drive a car, and wash the windows, and —"

"I say, sir," interrupted the young man hoarsely, "I came here to consult you about getting married. If I have to do all that, it's off!"

A Long Time

The company's employment office was checking on an applicant's list of references.

"How long did this man work for you?" a former employer was asked.

"About four hours," was the quick reply.

"Why, he told us he'd been there a long time," the astonished caller said.

"Oh, yes," answered the ex-employer, "he's been here two years."

Three Reasons

A small country church had raised some money, so the members called a meeting to determine how to spend it.

One member was emphatic in stating her case that the money should be used in buying a new chandelier. An old man, sitting in the back, was much opposed to it.

Finally the woman across arose and said, "Brother Jones, would you mind giving me one good reason why we shouldn't spend the money for a new chandelier?"

Brother Jones got up slowly, and said calmly, "Yes, I'll give you three. First, nobody can spell it so you can't order it. Second, nobody can play it. Third, we need better light."

Advice

A farm magazine received this letter from a reader:

"I have a horse that sometimes appears to be normal, and at other times is very lame. What shall I do?"

The publisher sent this reply:

"The next time your horse appears normal, sell him."

College

Son: "What is college bred?"

Pop: "My boy, they make college bred from the flour of youth and the dough of old age!"

Simpler

Mother began washing the face of her four-year-old son and he put up a strong fight.

"But you know I have to use soap and water to get you clean," his mother told him.

"Why can't you just dust me?" he asked.

Fish N' Chip

Two monks set up a fish 'n' chip stand in front of the monastery during the tourist season.

A woman asked one: "Are you the fish fryer?"

"No, ma'am," he replied, "I am the chip monk."

Old Family

The lady was trying to impress those at the party. "My family's ancestry is very old," she said. "It dates back to the days of King John of England." Then turning to a lady sitting quietly in a corner she asked condescendingly: "How old is your family, my dear?"

"Well," said the woman with a quiet smile, "I can't really say. All our family records were lost in the Flood."

Politeness

An old crossroads merchant wrote a debtor who had promised time and again to settle his long-delinquent account. The letter said:

"You are just a mule-eared liar. If you don't settle up. I aim to clobber you until there won't be nothing left but a pair of suspenders and a wart. I want my money and I want it now."

Then, remembering that even a collection letter should be polite, he added a postscript: "Please excuse the pencil."

The Poor Pedestrain

I gaze across the street so wide; I start, I dart, I squirm, I glide; I take my chances, oh, so slim—I trust to eye and nerve and limb. I scoot to right, I gallop through; I'm here and there, I'm lost to view.

My life, I know, hangs in the toss—another plunge—I am across! Oh, give me pity, if you can—I'm just a poor pedestrian!

Gruesome

Sign in a hotel: "Don't smoke in bed. The ashes that fall on the floor may be your own."

Changing Times

A Munich, Germany, hotel has posted a sign in each room: "Please be courteous to our employees. They are harder to get than guests."

Vice President

The city banker was visiting the countryside.

The banker, nodding toward a figure in the farmyard: "I suppose that's the hired man."

Farmer, with tongue in cheek: "Well, that's the first vice president in charge of cows."

Good Advice

"What do you think would go well with my new red slacks?" asked the overweight wife.

Answered the husband: "An ankle-length coat."

It Was Hard

Just imagine one of today's college graduates talking to his son 20 years from now: "Yes, sir, I started for a measly $800 a month and worked eight hours a day, five days a week!"

He Probably Does

A favorite story around the Atomic Energy Commission has to do with a group of nuclear scientists attending a meeting at Las Vegas. One of the scientists spent most of his time gambling recklessly at roulette.

"I'm shocked at the way Smith is throwing his money away at the gambling tables," one of the group told his colleagues. "He's gambling as if there were no tomorrow."

"Heavens!" exclaimed another scientist. "Maybe Smith knows something."

Experience

A college football game was going badly, and a man in the stands knew why.

"Look at that halfback!" he stormed. "He's fumbled three times. Why do they let a stupid moron like him play?"

His seven-year-old son regarded him with anxious eyes.

"Daddy," he reasoned, "maybe it's his football."

Expensive

"How shall I account for the ten thousand dollars our cashier skipped out with last week?" asked the bookkeeper.

"Oh, charge it to running expenses," directed the boss, after a moment's thought.

Sounds Alike

One of my 4th grade boys came to me to recite the books of the Old Testament. This is how it went, "Genesis, Exodus, Leviticus, Numbers, Astronomy."

Right

A tourist in New York City walked up to a resident who seemed to show some of the identifying marks of a beatnik. The tourist asked, "How do I get to Carnegie Hall?" The resident looked the tourist up and down, and then with a happy grin replied, "Practice, Man, Practice!"

A Bargain

Let me sell you a house by the side of the road. I've lived in the old thing for years. You'll like it a lot, it faces the spot where all the truck drivers change gears.

Like Father

Two modern little girls coming home from Sunday school were solemnly discussing the lesson.

"Do you believe there is a devil?" asked one.

"No," replied the other promptly, "of course not. It's just like Santa Claus. He's your father."—*Elberton Star*

Denomination

The story is told of a woman in Kansas who went into her local postoffice shortly after John Kennedy was elected president. When she asked the clerk for 50 cents worth of stamps, he asked, "What denomination?"

"Well, I didn't know it would ever come to that," she snapped angrily. "Baptist."

Different

A country pastor went to see one of his members who had not been in church the previous Sunday. "I had haying to do," the farmer explained. "It was over in the back field where no one could see me working on the Sabbath."

"But God saw you," the pastor reminded him. "Yes, I know that," replied the farmer, "but He's not as gossipy as the people around here."

Speakers

A physician reports the sense of hearing is considerably dulled by eating. Which is nature's way of protecting us against after-dinner speakers.

Double Duty

In a small town, the sheriff was also the veterinarian. One night he got a frantic phone call. "Do you want a sheriff or veterinarian?" he asked.

"Both," came the reply. "We can't get our dog's mouth open, and there's a burglar in it."

His Real Subject

Once there was a young minister who kept boring his congregation with sermon after sermon on baptism. Finally the church officers instructed him to preach on the subject of pills the following Sunday. They could see no connection between pills and baptism.

So on Sunday, the young minister announced that pills would be his topic for the day. "There are big pills and little pills," he said, "bitter pills and sweet pills, cheap pills and expensive pills. Another pill is the gospill—and that gets me to my real subject—'baptism.'"

Not Good Enough

"I say, Jones, if I were you I wouldn't let your wife go around saying she's made a man of you. You don't hear my wife saying that."

"No," Jones agreed, "but I've heard your wife telling my wife that she had done her best."

Grandmother

A little boy came home from Sunday school and could not remember the name of his new teacher. "But she was Jesus' grandmother," he added, startling his parents.

"How do you know that?"

"Why," he explained reasonably enough, "she talked about Him all the time and she kept showing us those big pictures of Him!"

He Had Missed Them

Game warden: "Say, you're hunting with last year's license."

Hunter: "Yeah, I know. But I'm only shooting at the ones I missed last year."

Frank

The application blank for a new driver's license carried the question, "Have you ever been arrested?" The applicant put down, "No."

The next question was, "State why?" The applicant answered, "Never been caught."

New Experience

The hostess at a children's birthday party was chatting with one of the little girls. "My, your younger brother is shy," she said. "He hasn't moved from that corner all afternoon."

"He's not shy," the little girl said. "He's never had a necktie on before and he thinks he's tied to something.

Didn't Need It

A woman went into a pet shop to buy a drinking trough for her dog. "Would you like one inscribed 'For the Dog?' " asked the proprietor.

"It really doesn't matter," she replied. "The dog can't read, and my husband doesn't drink water."

No Such Accommodation

The hotel reservation clerk opened the telegram and read:

"Do you have any accommodation where I can put up with my wife?"

Don't Look Now

Only a woman could ask: "Don't turn around, but who is that couple that just came in?"

No Experience

A father, buying a doll for his daughter's birthday, was told by the saleslady, "Here's a lovely doll—you lay her down and she closes her eyes, just like a real little girl."

"I guess," said the father sadly, "you've never had a real little girl."—*Arkansas Baptist*

Don't Get Lost

Boy Scout leader to troop: "Remember, men, if you're lost in the woods at night, get your bearings from the sky. A glow will indicate the nearest shopping center."

Membership

A lady told a church visitor recently that she was not ready for church affiliation "because there are so many abominations that I don't know which one I want to join."—*Tarrytown Tidings, Tarrytown Baptist Church (Austin, Texas)*

Not Positive

"Do you have a criminal lawyer in town?" a tourist asked an oldtimer.

"Well, we think so," the old man said, "but we can't prove it."

Fair

"Darling," scolded the mother. "You shouldn't always keep everything for yourself. I have told you before that you should let your brother play with your toys half of the time."

"I've been doing it," Darling replied. "I take the sled going downhill and he takes it going up."

Hard to Please

To honor Indian visitors at a club dinner, tablecloths of hand-woven, hand-printed Indian fabric were used.

"We hope it makes you feel at home," said a member to one of the Indian guests. The visitor smiled in acknowledgment, then voiced a complaint which husbands the world over will recognize.

"The difficulty is," he said, "I can't get my wife to use these. She thinks she has to have Irish linen."—*Robin Goodfellow, Cambridge (England) Daily News*

Gossip

A woman wrote to a newspaper from a lonely spot up in Alaska: "My sister and I aren't exactly lonely up here because we have each other to talk to. But we need another woman to talk about."

They Pay

In a Las Vegas restaurant a tourist played the slot machines. As fast as he ran out of coins, he would replenish them with change from the cashier. On his fourth such trip he demanded, "Don't any of these machines ever pay?"

"Oh, yes indeed, sir!" the cashier replied. "They pay the lights. They pay the rent. They pay the kitchen help. They pay me. They pay real good, sir."

Str8 Typography

There was a lad named Willie T8, who loved a lass called Annie K8. He asked if she would be his m8, but K8 said w8.

His love for K8 was very gr8—he told her it was hard to w8, and begged to know at once his f8—but K8 said w8.

Then in stepped f8, he grew sed8, and soon he hit a faster g8, and for another m8 went str8. Now K8 can w8!

Wrong Direction

A Mississippi river steamboat was stopped in the mouth of a tributary stream, owing to the dense fog. An inquisitive passenger inquired of the captain the cause of the delay.

"Can't see up the river," was his laconic reply.

"But I can see the stars overhead," the passenger said sharply.

"Yes," came back the captain, "but unless the boilers bust, we ain't goin' that way."

New Idea

"Well, John, how does it feel to be a grandfather?"

"Oh, it's good news, of course, but I'll have to get used to the idea of being married to a grandmother!"

Enjoy Yourself

Lady: "I'll give you a quarter, not because you deserve it, but because it pleases me to do so."

Hobo: "Thank you, ma'am, but couldn't you make it a dollar, and thoroughly enjoy yourself?"

Knew His Business

"Waiter," exclaimed the angry diner, "you've got your thumb on the steak!"

"Yeah," was the reply, "I don't want it to fall on the floor again."

Experience

During a bad electrical storm, a mother thought her young son would be frightened so she tiptoed into his room to comfort him.

The boy opened his eyes and mumbled: "What's Daddy doing with the television set now?"

He Wasn't Cheating

At the home talent golf tournament the club secretary saw one of the entrants driving off about a foot in front of the teeing mark.

"Here!" he cried. "You can't do that. You're disqualified!"

"What for?" demanded the golfer.

"Why, you're driving off in front of the mark."

"G'wan back to the clubhouse," he said tersely. "I'm playing my second stroke!"

Come and Get It

In a county newspaper appeared the following ad: "The man who picked up my wallet on Main Street was recognized. He is requested to return it."

In the next issue the reply was published: "The recognized man who picked up your wallet requests the loser to call and get it."

Friendly Spirit

Prof: "If there are any dumbbells in the room, please stand up."

A long pause. Then a lone Freshman stood up in the rear.

"What—do you consider yourself a dumbbell?" asked the Prof.

"Well, not exactly," replied the Freshman, "but I don't want to see you standing all alone."

O.K.?

Young Mrs. Curtis thrust her husband's paycheck through the window and asked the bank teller if he would please cash it.

The teller looked at the signature and saw that it was all right. "But the check needs an endorsement first," he told her.

Mrs. Curtis looked thoughtful for a moment, then wrote on the back of the check: "My husband is a wonderful man. Harriet Curtis."

Sorry

It was the first day on the job for the pretty blonde steno just out of school. Her boss picked up the first of her finished letters, and with a sigh said, "You can't spell very well, can you? I see you spelled sugar, s-u-g-g-e-r."

"Oh, dear, so I have!" she exclaimed. "How do you suppose I came to leave out the 'h'?"

High IQ

Feeling pretty discouraged with the work his new secretary was getting out, the boss decided to test her intelligence.

"Did you ever hear of Harding?" he asked.

"No," she answered.

"Hoover?"

"No."

"Lincoln?"

"I think so," she brightened. "Is his last name Nebraska?"

Say That Again, Please

In a swank photography studio a society matron was looking at a new picture she had had taken. "That picture is an outrage. Now, I ask you, does it look like me?"

The suave photographer bowed and said, "Madam, the answer is in the negative."

Perfectly Safe

A garage man answered the distress call of a woman motorist whose car was stalled. He made an examination and informed her it was out of gas.

"Will it hurt," she asked, "if I drive it home with the gas tank empty?"

Head of the Class

Professor: "Joseph, describe hibernation to the class."

Joe: "To hibernate is to pass the winter in a state of torpor, as do certain animals. It is a sort of suspended animation during which life flickers low, and the animal barely exists through the cold, dark part of the year."

Professor: "Correct. Give us an example."

Joe: "A baseball fan."

Too Long

The harsh, Scrooge-like boss berated his employee who was due at 8 but did not get in until 9.

"Look at me," said the employee, holding up a bandaged arm. "I fell out of a second story window."

The boss asked angrily, "Did that take an hour?"

Didn't Run Fast Enough

A Moscow radio told of the incredible series of records set by an athlete named Ivan Skorlovsky, who smashed all existing world records for the 200-yard dash, the mile run, the five-mile run, and the 100-mile run, overcoming such obstacles as a blizzard, a range of mountains, and lack of water.

"Unfortunately," added the announcer, "Skorlovsky's fantastic performance was in vain. He was captured and brought back to Moscow."

Service

A barber's sign in Laurelville, Ohio, reads: "Haircut While You Wait."

Either Way

At a railroad crossing near Colorado Springs, Colorado, appears this sign: "The average time it takes a train to pass this crossing is 14 seconds, whether your car is on it or not."

Best Seller

This request was received by the U. S. Fish and Wildlife Bureau: "Please send me a pamphlet on wildlife in our government."

Correct

A little girl returning from Sunday school was asked by her grandmother how many had been in her class that day. She replied: "Counting Jesus, there were fifteen of us."

—*Beatrice Plumb, Christian Herald*

Parable

Little Willie was asked if he ever studied the Bible.

"Yes, sir," he replied.

"Then of course you have read the parables?"

"Yes, sir," said Willie.

"Good," said the teacher. "And will you tell me which parable you like best?"

"I like the one where everybody loafs and fishes."

—*Southern Baptists' Brotherhood Journal*

Makes Sense

As a woman approached her car in a crowded parking lot, a policeman stopped her. "Your license plates are on upside down!" he exclaimed. "I know," she explained brightly. "It saves me a lot of time. Now I don't have to wander all over the parking lot looking for my car."

A Messed Up War

"Look at youse!" shouted the Army sergeant indignantly, as he glanced over a bunch of new and inexperienced recruits. "Your ties are crooked. Your hair ain't combed. Your shoes ain't polished. Your trousers ain't pressed. . . . Suppose some country suddenly declared war!"

Safety

A friend asked a young minister why he resigned from his first pastorate. "Because," said the young pastor, "there were 15 girls, widows and old maids there, all trying to marry me."

"But don't you know," asked the friend, "there is safety in numbers?"

"Not for me," the minister laughed, "I found mine in Exodus!"

Human Nature

The police station had been quiet all day and most of the week. The men were playing cards to pass the time.

"What a life," grouched one of the officers. "No fights, no burglaries, no riots, no nothin', not even a stabbing. If it stays this quiet, they'll reduce the force."

"Rest easy, Mike," said the captain, raising the pot. "Things will break soon. You've got to have faith in human nature."

Thanks Anyway

Niece: "Thanks very much, Uncle Wilbur, for my birthday gift."

Uncle Wilbur: "Oh, that's nothing to thank me for!"

Niece: "That's what I thought, but Mother told me to thank you anyway."

Right

"What goes 'oom, oom'?" asked Walter.
"A cow walking backward," replied David.

Don't Worry

Officer: "Why did you keep on going after I whistled?"
Driver: "Sorry, officer, I'm quite deaf."
Officer: "Well, don't worry, you'll have your hearing in the morning."

No, A Round Trip

"I want two reservations for a trip around the world," stated the millionaire.
"Yes, sir," said the clerk. "One way?"

No Worrier

"That fellow owes me $20."
"And won't he pay it?"
"Pay it! He won't even worry about it!"

Right Method

Professor: "If molecules can be split into atoms, and atoms broken up into electrons, can electrons be split up any further?"
Student: "Well, Professor, you might try mailing them to someone in a package marked 'Fragile.' "

It That Clear

She: "Why does the man behind the hitter wear such a big bib, honey? He looks silly."
He: "That, my dear, is to keep the catcher's shirt from getting all mussed up in case a ball happens to knock his teeth out."

Correct

A tourist was visiting New Mexico. While gazing at the dinosaur bones that were all over the place, he met an old Indian who acted as an official guide.

"How old are these bones?" asked the tourist.

"Exactly one hundred million and three years old," was the Indian's reply.

"How can you be so definite?" asked the tourist.

"Oh," replied the Indian, "a geologist told me they were one hundred million years old, and that was exactly three years ago."

Is That Nice

Father: "Don't you think Junior gets his intelligence from me?"

Mother: "He must have; I still have mine."

That's Different

Farmer: "Say, you've sure got a lot of nerve to come down in a parachute with this 100-mile-an-hour gale blowing!"

Camper: "I didn't come down in a parachute. I went up in a bloomin' tent!"

Times Change

"I hear that your son is getting on quite well."

"Oh, definitely! Only two years ago he was wearing my old suits. Now I wear his."

Foresight

Two foremen were comparing notes. "Do all the boys in your shop drop their tools the moment the whistle blows?" asked one.

"No, not at all," replied the other foreman. "The orderly ones have their tools all put away before that time."

And Frighten Everyone?

"Mother," said Charlie, "I'd like to ask you a question."
"Well, what is it, dear?"
"When a lightning bug lightens, why doesn't it thunder?"

He Lost

Phil: "How did you come out in the pie-eating contest?"
Bill: "Jimmy came in first and I came in sick."

Lucky It Wasn't 100 Feet High

Bob: "My brother went hiking the other day and while he was out in the woods he fell out of a tree fifty feet high."
Rob: "Was he badly hurt?"
Bob: "Oh, no, he had only climbed two feet when he fell."

What Happened?

Employer, to a boy half an hour late: "You should have been here at 8 o'clock."
Boy: "Why, what happened?"

No Fair

Two fishermen sitting on a bridge, their lines in the water, made a bet as to who would catch the first fish. One got a bite, and became so excited that he fell off the bridge.
"Oh, well," said the other, "if you're going to dive for them, the bet's off!"

Fortunate

Man: "Doctor, I have a corn on the bottom of my foot."
Doctor: "That's lucky. You're the only one that can step on it."

Understandable

Doctor: "You are overweight again, Mrs. Fuller. You haven't been keeping strictly to that diet I gave you."

Mrs. Fuller: "Well, no, doctor. After all I don't want to starve to death just for the sake of living a little bit longer."

That's Different

"Sorry we don't have potted geraniums," the clerk said, and then added helpfully, "Could you use African violets?"

"No," replied the man sadly. "It was geraniums my wife told me to water while she was gone.

Smart Student

Professor: "What is the difference between electricity and lightning, class?"

Student: "We don't have to pay for lightning."

His Secret

Cowboy: "Hey, you're putting the saddle on backwards!"

Dude: "You think you're so smart. You don't even know which way I'm going."

They Always Do

The young couple had had their first quarrel, and for several hours neither would speak to the other. Finally the husband decided to give in.

"Please speak to me, dear," he said. "I'll admit I was wrong and you were right."

"It won't do any good," sobbed the bride, "I've changed my mind."

He Made It

"I've already done my good deed for the day," said the Boy Scout to his father at breakfast.

"What," exclaimed the father, "before breakfast!"

"Yes," said the youngster, "when I saw that Johnny's father was late for the 7:30 train, I turned the dog loose. He made it."

And Clear?

The boss, leaving the office, was instructing his new secretary on what to say while he was out.

"I may be back before lunch," he told her. "And then again, I may not. I may not be back until tomorrow morning."

"Yes, sir," the secretary said. "Is that definite?"

He Was Really Certain

Office Clerk (nervously): "Please, sir, I think you're wanted on the phone."

Employer: "You think! Don't you know?"

Office Clerk: "Well, sir, the voice at the other end said, 'Hello, is that you, you old idiot?' "

Of Course

"I've just returned from a safari in Africa," bragged John.

"How was the hunting?" asked his stay-at-home friend.

"Not bad. I bagged some lions, a leopard, and a potfor."

"What's a potfor?"

"To cook in, silly!"

Sorry

"I'm sorry to be late, Mom," said ten-year-old Jimmy as he rushed home from school. "We were making a science display, and I had to stay to finish the universe."

Happy Resort

A sightseeing party was visiting Plymouth Rock. Viewing the marble canopy over it, and the delightful old hotel nearby, the wit of the party remarked, "I bet those Pilgrims were sure glad to have a place like that to clean up in after that long voyage."

Heap Big Winner

A deserted farmhouse in a gullied field was pictured in a farm magazine some time ago, and a prize was offered for the best 100-word description. The award was given to an Indian, who submitted the following:

"Picture show white man crazy. Cut down trees, Make big tepee. Plow hill. Water wash. Wind blow soil. Grass gone. Door gone. Window gone. Whole place gone. Buck gone. Papoose gone. Squaw too. No chuckaway. No pigs. No corn. No plow. No pony. Indian no plow land. Keep grass. Buffalo eat grass. Indian eat buffalo. Hide make tepee. Make moccasin. Indian make no terrace. No make dam. All time eat. No hunt job. No hitch hike. No ask relief. No shoot pig. Great Spirit make grass. Indian no waste anything. Indian no work. White man loco."

Exercise

The man who goes fishing on his vacation usually gets a lot of additional exercise when he gets home. He has to stretch his arms to their full length every time he meets a friend to show him the size of the fish that got away.

Getting Soft

With those electric tooth brushes, can openers, and dishwashers kids are getting soft. A parent gave a kid a bat to play with in a Little League game. The boy asked, "Where do I plug it in?"

That's Different

Hubby came home at 2 a.m. and the wife met him at the door: "Halt! Who goes there!" she asked.

"A friend," he answered.

"Advance friend and give the password."

"I won eighteen dollars," the man replied.

"Come in, darling." she said.

Is That Clear?

We can't pass up this opportunity to repeat Joe Schroeder's famous introduction of genial Bert Hoerr, when he first became a member. "He pronounces his name," said Joe, "hare, as in rabbit; or hair, as in soup."

She Knew

A friend of Anita Loos once said, "I always wondered how you could write 'Gentlemen Prefer Blondes' when you are a brunette."

"That's how I know," sighed Anita.

No Friends Then

Reporter: "After you inherited that fortune, were you bothered by friends you had when you were poor?"

Heir: "I never had any friends when I was poor."

Appreciative

The owner of a large department store was awakened at 3 a.m. in his home by a phone call. The voice at the other end identified himself: "I'm one of your customers. I bought a sofa in your store, and I want to tell you how beautiful it is."

The sleepy store owner replied: "I appreciate the compliment, but tell me, when did you buy this sofa from us?"

"I bought it from you four months ago."

"What? You bought it from us four months ago and you wake me up at three in the morning to tell me about it?"

"Yes—it just arrived!"

Sounds Reasonable

"Willie," said the teacher, "can you name the principal river of Egypt?"

"It's the Nile."

"That's right. Now can you tell me names of some of the smaller tributaries?"

Willie hesitated, then smiled. "The juveniles!"

Smart Boy

"I'm sorry, sir," said the boy learning to dive, "but I couldn't dive from the highest board. It's all of fifteen feet."

"I know, but you need to conquer your fear," answered the instructor firmly. "Supposing you were that high above the water on a sinking ship. What would you do then?"

"Wait for the ship to sink another ten feet, sir."

I'll Say Not

The young lady told her friend that she was going to marry a rather eccentric millionaire.

"But," her friend said, "everyone thinks he's a little bit cracked."

"He may be cracked," the young lady said, "but he certainly isn't broke."

Don't Worry

He rushed in the door exclaiming loudly, "Darling, I'm ruined. I've lost my job. I'm bankrupt. I haven't a cent."

His girl said soothingly, "Don't worry, sweetheart, I'll always love you—even if I never see you again."

That's Difficult

A first grade student asked his teacher how to spell "rat." Hiding her impatience, she gently spelled it for him.

Fixing her with a look of scorn, he replied: "I don't mean mousy rat. Anybody knows how to spell that. What I mean is like in 'Do it rat now.' "

Of Course Not

Customer (in restaurant): "A sardine sandwich, please."

Waiter: "Domestic or imported? The price is 35c for domestic, and 50c for imported."

Customer: "Domestic. I'm not paying any sardine's fare across the ocean!"

"Yes, Sir"

The general asked the computer, "Will there be war or peace?"

The computer flashed, buzzed, blinked, and said, "Yes."

"Yes, what?" roared the general.

The computer flashed, buzzed, blinked, then barked, "Yes, sir!"

Helpful

The departing baby-sitter said to the returning parents, "By the way, I promised Janie that if she went to bed, you'd buy her a pony in the morning."

Modern Child

"How do you do, my dear?" said the old lady to the little girl.

"Quite well, thank you," was the polite reply.

There was a pause and then the old lady asked. "Why don't you ask me how I am?"

"Because," said the child calmly, "I'm not interested."

They Came

The pastor, looking at the collection plate, mused: "I always said the poor are welcome here—and I see they have come."

American Way of Life

A refugee couple arrived in the United States several years ago with one dream—to become citizens. Through much red tape and years of study, they were patient and hopeful. Then one day the husband rushed into the kitchen with the long-awaited news.

"Anna! Anna!" he shouted. "At last. We are Americans!"

"Fine," replied the wife, tying her apron around him. "Now you wash the dishes."

On the Way Down

"There I was," the club bore explained to his fellow members, "with two lions making for me from different directions. I fired the right barrel and the first lion fell dead. Then I swung around and got the second lion with the left barrel. But before I could reload, an enormous buffalo charged out of the bush at me. Fortunately I was right beside a tree, with the lowest branch 15 feet from the ground. I leaped—"

"You're not going to tell us you jumped straight up and caught it?" interrupted a listener.

"Of course not," the bore replied, "I missed it on the way up, but I got it on the way down."

The Reason

Psychiatrists say that girls tend to marry men like their fathers. Now we know why mothers cry at weddings.

It Was Intense

Willie to the circus went, he thought it was immense; his little heart went pitter-pat for the excitement was in tents.

Names

General Sherman was once a guest at a banquet that was followed by a reception. Among the people who shook hands with him was a man whose face was familiar, but whom he could not place.

"Who are you?" the general asked in a whisper, as he heartily welcomed the guest.

The man's face flushed as he answered, "Made your shirts, sir."

"Ah, of course," exclaimed the general. Then turning to the receiving committee, he said, "Gentlemen, allow me to present Major Shurtz."

Mistake

An irate employee went to the paymaster's window at the plant and laid down his pay envelope. Carefully counting out the money, he looked the paymaster in the eye and said, "One dollar short."

The paymaster picked up the envelope and turned to a record sheet to check the amount due. Smiling broadly, he came back to the window. "Last week we overpaid you a dollar," he explained. "You didn't complain about that."

"An occasional mistake I can overlook," replied the angry employee, "but not two in a row."

Twins

More twins are being born these days. Maybe kids lack the courage to come into this world alone.

Fish Story

First Fisherman: "I tell you it was that long! I never saw such a fish."

Second Fisherman: "I believe you."

Space Costs

Bob—"Think there is any intelligent life on Mars?"

Rob—"There must be; you don't see them wasting $30 billion to find out about us."

Exception

Groucho Marx is a master of the retort discourteous. On his TV show he once told a guest: "I never forget a face—but in your case I'll make an exception."

That's Different

Wife to irate husband: "Normally I wouldn't dream of opening a letter addressed to you, but this one was marked 'private'."

Easy Mistake

The man down the hall says he's finally found the cause of his back trouble. Two weeks ago he got some of that ultra-modern office furniture, and he's just discovered he's been sitting all this time in his wastebasket.

Interesting Ride

Little boy to his mother after returning from a ride with his father: "We passed two idiots, three morons, four darn fools and I don't know how many knotheads."

Pedestrian

In the old days a man who died with his boots on was known as a "bad man." Now he's a pedestrian.

Smart Dog

A father, listening to his 7-year-old scratch away on his violin, while the dog howled dismally nearby, finally asked the boy, "Can't you play something the dog doesn't know?"

Close

You can't fool all of the people all of the time, but some of those super highway interchange signs come pretty close.

A Miracle

"Well, Doc," asked the applicant for an insurance policy, "how do I stand?"

"I don't know," replied the Doc. "It's a miracle."

Heard One—Saw One

A long time ago, in Houston, a man was murdered in front of our little college, about three blocks from the old San Jacinto Bridge. The only eyewitness was a janitor, Halley. During the trial, the judge said, "Halley, let's get this straight. You say these two men raced around the corner directly toward you, and you heard two shots, about three or four seconds apart."

Halley replied, "Yes, Judge, and the shots went bang . . . bang!"

The Judge asked, "Then you saw the defendant shoot the deceased in the back twice?"

"No sir, Judge. I saw the first shot. But that second shot . . . I heard it when I was crossing the San Jacinto Bridge."

Lost His Grip

Groucho Marx, lunching with Arthur Murray, grabbed for the check—and won. "Either you're losing your grip," Marx said, "or I don't know my own strength."

Baby

A father for the first time was sent to a dry goods store to purchase a dozen diapers. The clerk wrapped up the dozen diapers and handed them to the new father.

"How much?" asked the customer.

"$2.50 for the diapers and 25 cents for the tax," replied the clerk.

"I'll take the diapers," said the father, "but we intend using safety pins."

Wisdom

"Integrity and wisdom are essential to success in every business," said the boss to the new employee. "By integrity, I mean that when you promise a customer something, you must keep that promise, even if we lose money."

"And what is wisdom?" asked the new man.

"Don't make such fool promises!"

Hinges

The little girl was eating a chicken wing. She nibbled but finally asked her father, "May I have a different piece? This is all hinges."

Rights

All suburbanites are endowed with certain inalienable rights; among these are life, liberty, and the pursuit of crabgrass.

Power

Asked the secret of his power as a preacher, a minister in Chicago declared, "It's simple. I read myself full. I think myself clear. I pray myself hot. And then I let go."—*James Hines*

Foresight

The little old lady confidentially told her neighbor that she kept her money hidden at home in a coffee can.

"You know, of course," said the neighbor, "you are losing on your interest."

"Oh, no, I'm not," twinkled the little old lady, "I'm putting away a little extra just for that."

The Weather

A vacationer stopped at a country store and saw this sign: "This store will be closed August 20 on account of the weather."

As it was then only August 15, the traveler asked the proprietor how he could know what the weather would be in five days.

"Well," he said, "if she rains light, I'm goin' fishin'. If it's a heavy rain, I'm goin' to stay home and work on my tackle."

"But how do you know it's goin' to rain?" asked the visitor.

"Don't care if it rains or not," he snapped. "If it's sunny, I'll go fishin' or work on my tackle anyway. All depends on the weather."

He Lost

When James A. Farley was a director of the New York Central railroad, he found himself across the table from a patron of the road at breakfast. The man had ordered a breakfast which cost $1.45 and he gave the waiter two dollar bills.

A short time later the waiter came back with the change, a 50-cent piece and a nickle. The train rider studied the two coins for a time and, after some hesitation, picked up the 50-cent piece and left the nickle. Before he could get away the waiter came up. To the rider's surprise the waiter was grinning broadly. "That's all right, sir," he said. "I gambled and I lost."

Poor Salesmanship

Former President Dwight D. Eisenhower, who was fond of golf stories, liked the one about the tramp who crawled into a sand trap late one night and fell asleep in comfort. He slept rather late and was roughly awakened by several well delivered kicks.

"Cut it out," he yelled. "Who do you think you are?"

"I'm the chairman of the membership committee of this club," replied the kicker.

"O.K.," said the tramp, pulling himself up, "but all I have to say is this is a lousy way to get new members."

Shoe Store

Shoe department manager to customer: "Yes, we have quite a selection of loafers. I'll see if I can get one to wait on you."

Pedigree

"I want a dog of which I can be proud," said Mrs. Newly-rich. "Does that one have a good pedigree?"

"Lady," declared the kennel owner, "if he could talk, he wouldn't speak to either of us."—*Arkansas Baptist*

Not Deep Enough

Two Irishmen were digging a hole in the main street of the town, but apparently had dug up the wrong part of the street and were ordered to fill up the hole again. They did so and were dismayed when they found they had quite a large heap of earth left over.

"Shure, I told ye so," remonstrated Patrick. "I said all along we should 'ave dug this hole deeper."

Perfect Time

Former President Lyndon Johnson recalls that the late Senator Alben W. Barkley (D., Ky) used to tell about the fellow tn the Kentucky hills who had a cuckoo clock. Several nelghbors wanted him to get rid of it because it didn't keep good time.

"It keeps very good time," said the man. "When the hands point at two and the clock strikes four, it's half past six."

Don't Be Too Sure

A corporal reported to a new regiment with a letter from his captain saying, "This man is a great soldier, and he'll be even better if you can cure him of his constant gambling."

The new C.O. looked at him sternly and said, "I hear you're an inverterate gambler. I don't approve. It's bad for discipline; what do you bet on?"

"Practically anything, sir," said the corporal. "If you'd like, I'll bet you $20 that you've got a strawberry birthmark under your right arm."

The C.O. snapped, "Put down your money."

He stripped to the waist, proved conclusively he had no birthmark and pocketed the bills on the table. He couldn't wait to phone the captain and exult, "That corporal of yours won't be in such a hurry to make a bet after what I just did to him."

"Don't be too sure," said the captain mournfully. "He wagered me one hundred he'd get you to take your shirt off five minutes after he reported."

House Call

A psychiatrist saw another psychiatrist plodding down the street carrying a couch on his head.

"Why the couch?" he called after his colleague.

"House call," replied the burdened one.

A New Definition

"Pop," inquired little Clarence Lilywhite, "what is a millennium?"

"Sure," said the parent, "don't you know what a millennium is, child? It's just about like a centennial, only it's got more legs."

Vacation

"Mummy," said the little boy, "why does the minister get a month's holiday in the summer when Daddy only gets two weeks?"

"Well, son," answered Mother, "if he's a good minister, he needs it. If he isn't, the congregation needs it!"

Sounds Reasonable

"Now tell the court how you came to take the car," said the judge.

"Well," answered the accused, "it was parked in front of the cemetery, so I thought the owner was dead."

One of Those Days

On my way here, my car bumped into one that had a "Just Married" notice on it. There was no damage, but I apologized to the fellow inside anyway. He replied: "Oh, it doesn't matter. It's been one of those days!"

Small

The Sunday School teacher, seeking to bring home the story of the Star in the East compared with other stars in the sky, asked her first graders to count the number of stars they could see at night.

The next Sunday, the pupils came to class reporting answers as varied as "153" to "too many to count." All except Georgie. He answered positively: "three."

"But, Georgie," the teacher asked, "how is it you saw so few stars when the other children found so many?"

Georgie was nonplussed, but just for a minute. "Well," he said apologetically, "our backyard is awfully small."

Fishing

Lugging a huge fish, an angler met another fishing enthusiast whose catch consisted of twelve small ones. "Howdy," said the first man as he gingerly laid down his large fish.

The other fellow stared for a few moments and calmly responded, "Just caught one, eh?"

Zoo

Mother: "Now, children, why do you want me to play with you?"

Twins: "We're playing zoo, Mom, and we need somebody to play the lady who comes and feeds all the animals candy and peanuts."

Proof

The hit-and-run driver was brought to trial. His lawyer pleaded eloquently in his behalf. "Your Honor, the plaintiff must have been walking very carelessly. My client is a very careful driver. He has been driving a car for 15 years."

"Your Honor," shouted the counsel for the plaintiff, "I can prove that my client should win this case without further argument. He has been walking for 45 years."

Trustworthy

A church secretary was spending her summer vacation at the beach. She was sunning herself on the sand when a little boy, also in a swimming suit, came up to her and asked: "Say, Miss, do you believe in God?" She answered: "I certainly do.

l believe in God with all my heart." Then he asked: "Well, do you go to church every Sunday?" She said: "I certainly do. I go to church every Sunday." Then he asked: "Do you read your Bible every day?" She said: "I do, son. I read my Bible every day." "Good," he said, "Will you hold my quarter? I'm going to take a swim."

Biblical Boners

Matt. 26:41 "The spirit indeed is willing, but the flesh is drowsy."

Matt. 13:34 "The stories by means of which Jesus taught were called parodies."

Matt. 6:34 "Sufficient unto the day is the evil eye."

Acts 9:3 "Saul saw the light, and was converted, on the road to recovery."

1 Cor. 13:12 "For now we see through a glass eye."

Rev. 6:8 "The four horsemen appear in the Acropolis."

Gen. 32:24 "Jacob wrestled all night with insomnia."

Gen. 41:27 "The seven thin cows in Pharaoh's dream meant no milk."

Signs

Outside an auto repair shop: "May we have the next dents, please?"

In a bookstore, going out of business, "Words failed us."

In a Volkswagen factory: "Think BIG and you're fired!"

In the window of a company gone bankrupt: "Opened by mistake."

A greenhouse: "Business is blooming."

Specialization

Bishop Fulton J. Sheen: "Specialization has reached such a state today that patients have to learn to diagnose themselves before they know which specialist to call."

Sounds Better

"Mal De Mer," explained Maurice Chevalier to a young lady about to take her first ocean voyage, "is merely a Frenchman's way of saying 'You can't take it with you.'"

Often Happens

Boy: "Since I met you I can't eat, I can't sleep, and I can't drink."

Girl (coyly): "Why not?"

Boy: "I'm broke."

Not Embarrassing

The young lady eyed her escort with great disapproval. "That's the fourth time you've gone back for more ice cream and cake, Albert," she said acidly. "Doesn't it embarrass you at all?"

"Why should it?" the hungry fellow shrugged. "I keep telling them I'm getting it for you."

Salesman

The store clerk had broken all sales records. Disclaiming credit, he explained to his boss, "A customer came in, and I sold him some fishhooks. 'You'll need a line for those hooks,' I said, and sold him some line. Then I told him, 'You have to have a rod to go with the line,' so I sold him a rod. 'You ought to have a boat so you can use your new rod in deep water,' I suggested, and sold him a boat. Next I told him, 'You'll need a boat trailer,' and he fell for that, too. Finally, I said, 'How will you pull the trailer without a car;' And guess what? He bought my car."

"But I assigned you to the greeting card department," said the boss.

"That's right," the salesman nodded. "This customer came in for a get-well card for his girl, who had a broken hip. When I heard that, I said to him, 'You haven't got anything to do for six weeks, so you might as well go fishing.'"

Sleep

Now I sit me down to sleep
The speaker's dull, the subject deep.
If he should stop before I wake
Give me a poke, for goodness sake.—*Anonymous*

Different View

A veteran salesman asked a fledgling, "How are you getting along?"

"Rotten, I got nothing but insults every place I called."

"That's funny," the old man mused. "I've been on the road forty years. I've had doors slammed in my face, my samples dumped down in the street; I've been tossed down stairs, been manhandled by janitors—but insulted? Never!"

To the Point

All the children were studying Greek history in the schools. After a few weeks they were asked to write an essay on all they had learned. The prize was won by a little Mexican girl whose composition consisted of three sentences: "The Life of Socrates." 1) Socrates was a Greek. 2) He went around giving advice to people. 3) The people poisoned him.

Needed Him

A lady went to the governor of her state and said to him, "Governor, I want to get my husband out of prison."

The governor asked, "What is he in prison for?"

She replied, "For stealing a ham."

The governor asked, "Is he a good husband?"

She replied, "No, sir. He drinks, he beats the children and he is no good."

Then the governor asked, "Why do you want him out of jail, if he is no good?"

She replied, "Well, governor, the fact is that we are out of ham again."

No Election

A gangling young man went to the county clerk's office and asked for a marriage license.

"Where's the bride elect?" asked the clerk.

"What d'ya mean bride elect?" said the young man. "There was no election. She appointed herself."—*Harvard Crimson*

I'll Say So

Eagle Scout: "Did you fish with flies while at camp?"

Tenderfoot: "We sure did! We fished, cooked, ate, slept, and hiked with flies."

It Happens

A man went down to Washington, his needs were simply stated; he had a simple problem but they made it complicated.

Who's Who In Sneezeland

"Where are you going, my pretty maid?" "I'm going to sneeze, kind sir," she said. "At who? At who? At who?" said he. "At-choo! At-choo! At-choo!" said she.

Usual Experience

He took her hand in marriage, but made a basic blunder of letting her retain a thumb to keep him under.

Not an Excuse

A young man called for military service sent his draft board the following excuse: "Convalescing from traumatic perisynovitis of the flexor digitorum sublimus in profundus muscle at the metacarpophalangeal joint." But the draft board batted not an eye. No, they said, a sore finger is no excuse!

Warning

"Anyone found near my chicken house at night," reads a notice in a country newspaper, "will be found there the next morning."

Time to Get Up

It was early morning and the husband whispered to his wife: "Must be time to get up."

"Why?" she asked.

"Because the baby just went to sleep."

No Brownie

Four-year-old sister: "When I grow up I'm going to be a Brownie."

Three-year-old brother (after a long period of thinking): "When I grow up I'm going to be a peanut butter and jelly sandwich!"

Decisions

I make all the big decisions in my family, and my wife makes the small ones. She decides whether to buy a car, whether we are going out, and I make the big ones—like whether to admit Red China to the U. N.—*George Gobel*

Playing It Safe

"Carl, why do you always lean out of the window while I'm practicing my violin?" asked his big sister.

"I don't want my neighbors to blame me," was the brother's impudent reply.

Considerate

While working on a log drive, a lumberjack fell into the water. Dizzy and nearly exhausted, he managed to grasp a big log and hold onto it. The current was so strong and swift that it swept his body under the log until his feet stuck out on the other side.

Just as a comrade, who had run to his assistance, grabbed him by the shoulders, he caught sight of his own feet protruding on the other side of the log.

"I can hold on a bit longer, Jim," he gasped. "Save the fellow who's in head first."

New Idea

Little Carol met the minister as she came out of a drugstore with an ice cream cone.

"Why didn't you give your money to the missions?" asked the minister.

"Oh," she replied, "I figured out a better way. I buy the ice cream cones and let the druggist give the money to the missions."

No Exaggeration

A producer of plays decided he was fed up with the extravagant ballyhoo in the advertising of so many shows. He insisted upon a clause in his contract which gave him the right to approve all advertising for a new play he was producing.

Writer after writer tried to make up an ad embodying the honesty and sincerity which he said he must have in his ads.

Finally one man brought a piece of copy which read like this: "Here is a play which combines the drama of Shakespeare, the wit of Rostand, the strength of Tennessee Williams, the intellect of Marlowe, and the plot mystery of Dickens. Greater than Hamlet, more moving than the Bible, this is a play destined to live forever."

"That's it," shouted the producer. "No exaggeration! Just the simple truth."

All Over

Two old ladies decided to take in the first football game of the season. They watched the kickoff and the various plays throughout a scoreless first half.

When the teams lined up for the second-half kickoff, one of them turned to the other and said, "It's time to go home. This is where we came in."

It Depends

"Where is Jimmy today?"

"If he knows as much about canoes as he thinks he does, he is out canoeing, but if he doesn't know any more about them than I think he does, he's swimming."

Her Prayer

Mary had been naughty and was sent into the bedroom to "think things over." After a while she came out all smiles and said, "I thought and I prayed."

"Fine!" said her mother. "That will help you to be good."

"Oh, I didn't ask Him to help me to be good," she said. "I told Him to help you put up with me."

Only In Texas

A Texan was visiting in the Alps. A native, wishing to show off his country, took him to a certain spot, gave a loud cry, and waited. After about six minutes, the echo came back clearly. "I'll bet you don't have anything like that in your country!" he said triumphantly.

"Oh, I wouldn't say that," said the Texan. "At our summer place in the hills, I just lean out the window before going to bed and yell, 'Hey, wake up' and eight hours later the echo wakes me."

Smart Parrot

A man bought a parrot and in trying to make him talk he kept repeating, "Hello! Hello!"

Finally, the parrot opened one sleepy eye and asked, "What's the matter? Line busy?"

It Might Help

Chairman of a banquet to the photographer: "Don't take his picture while he is speaking. Shoot him before he begins."

Absent-Minded

Householder: "Well, I see you brought your tools with you."

Plumber: "Yeah, I'm getting more and more absent-minded every day."

Next Question

Examiner: Who was your mother before she was married?
Applicant: I didn't have any mother before she was married.

Hard Question

After studying her son's latest examination results, a Sussex (England) wother told him he shows every sign of becoming a complete moron.

The boy nodded agreement. "What," he asked, "do you attribute it to—heredity or environment?"

Resemblance

"Your baby certainly is a cute little rascal," said the admiring visitor. "Does he take after his father?"

"In a way," answered the mother. "His father is not quite as cute—but more of a rascal."

No Need for Him

During a fire which was spreading rapidly through a Manhattan apartment building the tenants were rushing out into the street carrying their prized possessions. One lady noticed that the gentleman who lived directly over her was carrying a huge covered bird cage. "What have you got there?" she shouted.

"That's my pet rooster," he answered and the lady promptly fainted.

When she recovered, she was asked why she had fainted over such a trivial answer. "Well," she replied, "for several months I have been treated by a psychiatrist—because I kept hearing a rooster crowing."

She Reads Slowly

"Don't bother me for a moment. I'm writing to my little sister," said the Boy Scout at camp.

"Well, hurry up. Why are you writing so slowly?" said another Scout impatiently.

"She's little and can't read very fast yet."

Same Old Story

Little boy upon being introduced to an old friend of the family: "How do you do? My, how I have grown! May I go now?"

He Found Out

Genial general manager to new office boy: "Well, my lad, how are you getting on? Do you think you will like the business?"

Boy: "Oh, yes, sir."

Manager: "Well, don't forget the chief qualities we need in this office are brains and energy."

Boy: "Yes, sir; I have been here only two weeks, but I have found that out."

Webster Does the Work

Webster has the words, and I pick them up from where they lie; here a word and there a word—it's so easy, 'tis absurd. I merely 'range them in a row, Webster's done the work, you know; word follows word, 'til inch by inch, I have a column. What a cinch! I take the words that Webster penned and merely lay them end to end.

Of Spring We Sing

Spring is not the best of seasons. Colds and flu are two good reasons; wind and rain and other sorrow, warm today and cold tomorrow. Whoever said Spring was romantic? The word that best applies is frantic!

Many of Us Have

"I'd move heaven and earth to be able to break 100 on this course," sighed Mac, the golfer.

"Try heaven," advised the caddie. "You've already moved most of the earth."

No Other Service Needed

A man was seated in the barber chair getting a shave. The barber was comparatively new, and he nicked the customer badly. After he had finished the shave, the barber asked: "Do you want your head wrapped in a hot towel?"

"No," the exasperated customer replied, "I'll carry it home under my arm!"

Shop Early

Now that Santa Claus is on the horizon, the tidy people who mailed their Christmas cards last October have a problem. The stores are so thronged with shoppers these people are unable to buy their Easter egg dyes now.—*Hal Boyle*

Difficult to Service

A wealthy Texan, just back from a trip to Europe, met a friend in Houston.

"Welcome back," the friend said. "Did you pick up a Picasso or a Van Gogh?"

"No," replied the Texan. "They all have left-handed drives and besides you can't get parts for 'em anymore."

Good Question

A man who usually takes a bus to work overslept one morning and decided to drive. As he opened the garage door he saw that the rear wall—the one his wife smashed when she stepped on the gas pedal instead of the brake—had not been repaired. He called a carpenter after going back into the house. "You said that you would have it fixed by noon yesterday," he stormed.

"Let me ask you one question," said the carpenter quietly. "Did your wife drive the car in the afternoon?"

Look at the Jail-Birdie

The bank robber shoved a note across to the teller which read: "Put the money in a bag, sucker, and don't make a move."

The teller pushed back another note: "Straighten your tie, stupid. They're taking your picture."

Thank Goodness

Toward the end of the opera, Satan was thrusting Faust through a trapdoor which represented the gates of Hades. His majesty got through all right, he was used to going below, but Faust, who was quite stout, got only half way in, and no squeezing would get him any further. Suddenly a wit in the gallery exclaimed devoutly, "Thank God, Hell is full!"

Winter

Winter continues to impose on man. The father who used to wade through snow drifts to get to the cow barn, may have a son who braves the elements to reach the ski-lift.—*Douglas Meador, Matador Tribune*

Same Problem

A husband, whose relations were far from rosy, returned home one evening to find his young son sitting on the porch step with head in hands and a forlorn expression on his face.

"Well, what's wrong with you, Ronnie?" asked the boy's father.

There was a minute of silence; then the lad confessed, "Just between me and you, dad, I can't get along with your wife, either."

Then What?

Vladimir is on his way to the stadium and meets Ivan. He induces him to come along. When they arrive, the hammer throw event is taking place. Vladimir urges Ivan to try his prowess. Ivan dofts his coat, winds up, and tosses the hammer farther than it has ever been thrown before. The crowd rushes onto the field and congratulates him.

"That was nothing!" says Ivan. "Wait till you see how far I throw the sickle!"

Words

A university student asked the librarian for some information on euthanasia. The librarian disappeared, then returned with the comment: "I can't find anything dealing strictly with youth in Asia, but I found a book on youth in India."

Really Big

A western rancher had asked the district superintendent that a pastor be assigned to his community.

"How big a man do you want?" asked the superintendent.

"Well, Elder," the wiry man of tan replied, "we're not overly particular, but when he's on his knees we'd like to have him reach heaven."—*Doorstep Evangel*

Certainly Not

A patient consulting a psychiatrist learned that the fee would be $50 an hour, so in advance he wrote a $500 check for ten hours' treatment. When the psychiatrist looked at the check, he was amazed to see it was signed "Napoleon."

"Of course," said the patient. "If I signed my real name—would I need you?"

Easy to Understand

The weary husband was met at the door with sad news. "We'll have to go out for dinner," his wife said cheerily. "I couldn't fix anything because the electricity went off."

"Electricity," growled the husband. "We have a gas range."

"I know," the wife went on, "but we have an electric can opener."—*Arkansas Baptist*

A Difference

A schoolmaster had developed a reputation for short reports to parents. On one occasion he wrote of a certain boy. "Trying."

The parents were delighted—until the next report came in. This one read, "Very trying."

Pretty Bad

Overheard in East Berlin:

Two collective farmers are talking thinks over.

"How will the harvest pan out this year, comrade?" one of them asks.

"Middling," answers the other.

"What do you mean by that?"

"Worse than last year, but better than next."

Acoustics Are Bad Too

When the Bishop of Woolwich, England, author of "Honest to God," arrived to preach at a cathedral where he had not been heard before, the verger said to him: "You'll have to speak up, m'lord. The agnostics here are something terrible."

—*Peterborough*

The Answer to Him Is "No"

Sylvia: "When I applied for a job, the manager had the nerve to ask if my punctuation was good!"

Mildred: "What did you tell him?"

Sylvia: "I said I'd never been late for work in my life."

New Status

An advertiser in the *Times* of London last week put a Swedish-built sports car on the market with the words: "Status symbol for sale. Owner unfortunately changing status."

In the Army Now

The draftee was awakened roughly by his platoon sergeant after the rookie's first night in the army barracks.

"It's four-thirty!" roared the sergeant.

"Four-thirty!" gasped the sleepy recruit. "Man, you'd better get to bed. We've got a big day coming up tomorrow."

It Makes a Difference

Teacher: "If your mother gave you a large apple and a small one, and told you to divide with your brother, which would you give him?"

Joe: "You mean my little brother or my big one?"

As We See It

Stubbornness we deprecate, but firmness we condone. The former is our neighbor's trait, the latter is our own.

Spoiled the Sermon

John Wesley once preached a sermon in which he declared, "Get all you can." An old man exclaimed, "Amen."

"Keep all you can." Another "Amen" from the old fellow.

"Give all you can." The old man mumbled, "What a shame to spoil a good sermon."

He Did

The third-grade teacher was giving writing hints. "Don't copy what other people write," she said. "Be original. Write what's in you."

Little Tommy followed her advice. He wrote, "In me, there is a stomach, a heart, two apples, one piece of pie, and a lemon drop."

This Explains It

It has just been discovered that the reason Robin Hood stole from the rich was because the poor didn't have any money.

Bulletin

Bulletin in front of a church: Come in and get your faith lifted.

Cold Winter

It was terribly cold last winter. One day the newspaper would say snow, and the next day it would say cloudy. I shoveled two feet of "cloudy" off my sidewalk four times last winter.—*Red Blanchard*

Of Course Not

One of my grandchildren came home a few days ago and said the teacher had asked the first grade class what Noah did during the flood, and none of them seemed to know.

She asked, "Do you suppose that he fished?"

One bright little fellow held up his hands and said, "Teacher, you mean with just two worms?"—*Allan Shivers*

Inflation

"I feel sorry for the Joneses."

"Why?"

"With all the inflation, they can hardly keep up with themselves."

Not Necessary

My wife went down to the neighborhood pet store not long ago and bought a little drinking trough for the dog. As she started out with it, the storeowner said," Mrs. Shivers, don't you want me to paint on the side of it 'For The Dog'?"

She said, "No, it really doesn't matter. The dog can't read, and my husband doesn't drink water."—*Allan Shivers*

Explanation

The children were in a free-for-all when Dad entered the room. "Billie, who started this?" he asked the nearest boy.

"Well," replied Billie, "It all started when Frank hit me back."

Business

The retailer had ordered a large quantity of merchandise from a distributor. Back came this wire, "Cannot ship until you pay your last consignment."

Whereupon the retailer wired (collect, of course), "Unable to wait that long. Cancel the order."

Ignorance

"What is ignorance?" the teacher asked Eddie.

Answered little Eddie: "Ignorance is when you don't know anything and then somebody finds out."

Rank

The professor was annoyed when the student fresh out of the army was late to class for the third straight time. "Glad you could make it," he observed sarcastically. "Tell me, what did they say in the army when you showed up late?"

"Well," the student replied, "first they saluted. Then they asked, 'How are you this morning, Captain?'"

The Result

Take an average woman at a kitchen sink. Tell her to drop her dishmop and go to the beauty parlor. When she has received the full treatment, suggest that she buy a party dress and silver slippers. Then refer her to an expert who can choose the cosmetics that will enhance her personality. As a finishing touch, buy her an orchid. So, in only a few hours, what do you have? You have a glamour girl—and a sinkful of dirty dishes.

They're Not Speaking

At a sales convention in a distant city, one delegate received a letter, which he opened, and quickly threw in a waste basket.

"Who's it from?" asked a friend.

"From my wife."

The other picked up the letter and looked at it. "But this is a blank page. There's nothing written on it."

"I know," said the first man. "My wife got mad when I told her I was coming to the convention without her. Now we're not speaking."

Christmas

A veteran father says he intends to assemble a Christmas toy using nothing but the extra parts he has left over from toys he assembled on other Christmases.

Nothing Wrong

Laundryman: "But Madam, what's wrong with that lace tablecloth?"

Housewife: "Nothing, except it was a sheet when you took it."

He Will Get Well Soon

One of those legendary Texas tycoons wandered into a Cadillac agency to inspect the new models and was immediately approached by a salesman, order book in hand.

"May I help you?" he asked.

"Maybe you can, son," boomed the tycoon. "You see, I have this friend in the hospital. What've you got in the way of a get-well car?"

Typical Sergeant

Young Officer: "Sergeant, pick me out a nice, gentle horse."
Sergeant: "Have you ever ridden before?"
Officer: "No."
Sergeant: "Well, here's just the animal for you. Never been ridden before. You can both start together."

Baby

Lady: "Has your baby brother started to talk yet?"
Boy: "Oh yes, and now we are teaching him to keep quiet."

Rose

"Say, Bill," asked Tom, "how did you get that swelling on your nose?"

"Oh," said Bill, "I bent down to smell a brose in my garden."

"You mean a rose, don't you? There's no 'b' in a rose."

"There was in this one."

Speech

A farmer gave the young preacher this advice after listening to 30 minutes of fragments and pieces of thoughts whirling around in a high wind: "Son, don't you think it would be better to bale your hay before you deliver it?"

Be Careful

Instead of the usual "Keep Off the Grass" signs, those posted around the lawn of an operations building at an air base in France read: "When Crossing This Area Maintain An Altitude of 15 Inches."

Rank

A regular Army unit adopted as mascot an amiable bulldog who was named "Sergeant" and had three stripes duly sewn on his blanket.

One day the pooch chewed up a stack of vital documents. "Why didn't you stop him?" roared the officer n charge.

"I didn't dare," the clerk answered. "He outranks me."

Yes

"I'm not strictly a 'yes man' to my boss. When he says, 'No,' I say, 'No,' too!"

Slight Oversight

Those who sometimes give way to very high spirits on festive occasions should remember poor Joe and take it easy. Joe came home from a late party, roared into his driveway and smashed through the garage doors. As his neighbors said afterwards: "It's a good thing Joe didn't have his car."

Next Question

The job applicant tried his best to fill out the employment form. On the line asking, "Length of residence at present address," he thought and thought, and finally wrote: "About forty feet not counting the garage."

Commandments

A man told Mark Twain that it was his life's ambition to visit the Holy Land to see where Moses received the Ten Commandments from God. Mark Twain, knowing the man's habits, said, "Why don't you stay home and keep the Ten Commandments?"—*Robert W. Youngs, Christian Herald*

He Knew

"I don't agree that brunettes are any sweeter of disposition than redheads or blondes."

"Why?" asked a friend.

"My wife's been all three," replied the first, "and I can't see any difference."

Modern Youth

From a little girl's version of "The Three Bears:"

"And then the Papa Bear came home and said: 'Who ate up my porridge and left the TV on?' "

Not Becoming

One day, as he sat at a table after dinner, George Washington complained that the fire burning on the hearth behind him was too hot.

"But General," rejoined one of the guests, "it should behoove you, in your position, to stand fire."

"It does not become a general to receive it from the rear," came the instant reply.

Specialization

As the two surgeons were leaving the operating room, one turned to the other and said, "That was a close one, An inch either way and I would have been out of my specialty."

Two Troubles

The middle-aged woman went to see her doctor.

"Doctor," she said, "it's backache, shooting pains in my legs and bilious attacks."

"How old are you?" queried the physician.

"I shall be thirty-two on my next birthday," she calmly replied.

"Hm," said the doctor, busy writing, "and loss of memory, too."

Practical

Former Vice-President Garner had lost a ten-dollar bet on a baseball game, and the winner asked him to autograph the bill. "I'm giving it to my grandson for a souvenir," he explained. "He wants to frame it and hang it in his room."

"You mean the money's not going to be spent?" asked the Texan.

"That's right."

"Well," said Garner, "then I'll just write you a check!"

Come In Anyway

An Army chaplain, in an effort to reach more men, put this sign on his door: "If you have troubles, come in and tell us about them. If you haven't any, come in anyway and tell us how you manage."

Or a Student Driver?

The teacher, lecturing on perseverance, said: "He drove straight to his goal. He looked neither to the right nor to the left, but pressed forward, moved by a definite purpose. Neither friend nor foe could delay him, nor turn him from his course. All who crossed his path did so at their own peril. What would you call such a man?"

Student (quickly): "A truck driver!"

Try This One

On a patriotic occasion a young chemist, who did not know the first words of America, sang this synthetic substitute: "Cy-clo-hex-y-lam-ine, Pa-ra-len-can-a-line, Ben-zen-o-phone! Hy-dro-cy-an-im-ide, Sal-i-cyl-al-de-hyde, Tet-ra-car-bon-brom-ide, Hy-dro-quin-one!"

Still Doubtful

"Do you behave in church?" an interested relative asked Junior when he came to visit.

"I guess I do," said Junior. "I heard a lady behind me say she never saw a child behave so."

Bad When It's Quiet

Husband to wife: "I'll say this for television—the more unsuitable the program, the quieter it keeps the children!"

Good Sale

A youngster walked into a bank and said he had twenty-five dollars and wanted to open an account. The teller smiled and asked him how he had accumulated so much money.

"I've been selling magazine subscriptions," said the boy.

"Well, you've done very well," praised the teller. "Lots of people must have bought subscriptions from you."

"Nope," answered the boy proudly, "only one family—the dog bit me."

All Beach

An American tourist was in his bathing suit in the middle of the desert. An Arab rode by and blinked in amazement.

"I'm going swimming," the tourist explained.

"But the ocean's 800 miles from here," said the Arab.

"Eight hundred miles!" exclaimed the tourist. "Boy! What a beach!"

Not Very Old

A collector of antiques passed through a small town in Illinois one day and stopped to watch an old man splitting some logs. "That's a very old ax you have there," he volunteered.

"Yes," replied the old man, "and it once belonged to Abe Lincoln."

"You don't say!" exclaimed the collector. "But it doesn't look quite that old."

"Well," said the old man, "it ain't exactly. It's had four new handles and two new heads since Lincoln had it."

No Doubt About It

The wealthy playboy had been showing his guests the trophies he had brought back from a hunting expedition in India. Indicating a tiger-skin rug, he said, "When I shot this tiger it was a case of him or me!"

One of the rather uncultured guests stared at the tiger skin, and then at the host. "Well, old boy," he declared, "he sure makes a better rug!"

Good Recipe

Woman to bridge-club members: "I have the most marvelous recipe for goulash—all I have to do is mention it to my husband and he says, 'Let's eat out.' "

Dangerous Fellow

Employer: "I've had my eye on you, Johnson, and I see you're a hard worker. You keep long hours, you are ambitious, and you are rapidly learning the business."

Johnson: "Thank you, sir."

Employer: "So I'm obliged to discharge you. It's men like you who go out and start competing companies."

Well Evened Up

Things are pretty well evened up in this world. Other people's troubles are not as bad as yours, but their children are a lot worse.

Smart Fellow

"Young man," said the angry father from the head of the stairs, "didn't I hear the clock strike four when you brought my daughter in?"

"You did," admitted the boyfriend. "It was going to strike eleven, but I grabbed it and held the gong so it wouldn't disturb you."

The father muttered, "Wonder why I didn't think of that one in my courting days!"

He Sure Will

A West Texan pulled up in front of Houston's Shamrock Hotel in a cruiser-length car. He fished a ten-dollar bill out of his pocket and handed it to the doorman. "Take good care of the car," he said patronizingly.

"I sure will," answered the doorman. "I own one myself."

A Real Nip

"In your advertisement you said that there was a nip in the air after sundown," complained the tourist.

"Well," replied the resort owner, "take a look at those mosquitoes."

Worthwhile

Smithers announced to the boys at the office that he had started keeping bees as a hobby.

"Say, how do you like keeping bees?" a co-worker asked some time later.

"Just fine," replied Smithers happily. "We haven't had much honey but the bees have stung my brother-in-law several times."

Please Explain

Little Janie was sitting on her grandfather's knee one day and after looking at him intently for some time, she asked:

"Grandpa, were you in the ark with Noah?"

"Certainly not, my dear," he replied in astonishment.

"Then," said the child, "why weren't you drowned?"

Work

An over-worked farmer, on being asked what time he got up to go to work, replied, "Man, I don't go to work; I wake up in the middle of it."—*H. Gear, Hoard's Dairyman*

Or Republicans?

Little Jane's diplomacy was proved one day when she found that she and her three playmates all belonged to different faiths. One was a Lutheran, one a Presbyterian, one a Methodist, and she was a Catholic.

Before her mother could offer words of wisdom, Jane settled it.

"It really doesn't matter if we all go to different churches, just as long as we are all Democrats!"

Lies

The young mother was shocked to learn that little Sammy had told a falsehood. Taking the lad on her knees, she graphically explained the consequences of lying: "A tall, dark man," she began, "with red fiery eyes and two sharp horns grabs little boys who tell falsehoods and carries them off at night. He takes them to Mars where they have to work hard in a dark canyon for fifty years. Now, you won't tell a falsehood again, will you, Sammy?"

"No, ma'am," replied the lad, "you tell 'em better than I can."

Smart Judge

A reckless speeder was hauled before a judge in a traffic court recently.

The judge delivered quite a sermon, but the lady driver was not having any of it.

"Aren't you the eloquent one?" she sneered. "I'll bet you can recite Lincoln's Gettysburg Address by heart, too."

"I'm proud to say I can," admitted the judge, "and I hereby fine you fourscore and seven bucks."

CHAPTER 4

STORIES WITH INTERESTING FACTS

Seward's Folly

It was in 1867 that William Seward, then Secretary of State, persuaded a reluctant Congress to ratify the treaty with Russia which made Alaska a possession of the United States. The purchase price of $7,200,000 was considered exorbitant even though it figured about $12 per square mile, or less than 2 cents an acre. Upon discovery of the gold fields in the 1880s, "Seward's Folly" was acknowledged as a masterpiece of foresightedness. "Alaska Day," commemorating the purchase, is celebrated by the residents on October 18.

Young or Old?

People do not always consider that a person is young or old according to the number of calendar years that have passed. Their occupations seem to have a lot to do with it. A United States senator and a prominent baseball player were among the guests at a dinner recently. The newspapers referred to the 38-year-old ball player as "aging," and the 42-year-old senator as "boyish."

The Automobile in 1894

In 1894, when there were only four automobiles in the United States, a New York publisher brought out the first issue of the Horseless Age, a trade magazine, which contained this prophetic statement:

" . . . Those who have taken the pains to search·beneath the surface for the great tendencies of the age see what a giant industry is struggling into being."

Four years later, in 1898, a Massachusetts manufacturer made the announcement that 50 automobiles had been produced and sold in a 12-month period. In quick succession, a "stable" for renting, selling, storing, and repairing motor vehicles was opened in Boston; an automotive show was held in Manhattan; and a firm to buy and sell used motor cars was established there also that year.

Medieval Hospitality

The phrase "giving a cold shoulder" has a nutritional connotation. It dates back to medieval customs in French mansions. Then welcome and honored guests were served hot meat dishes, but when they overstayed their welcome or became otherwise unpopular, their host gave them a cold shoulder of beef or mutton.

Paper

Parchment, as a writing material, was developed in the ancient town of Pergamon in Asia Minor. Incidentally, Pergamum is the third of the seven churches in the Book of Revelations. The Apostle Paul labored there. The Ptolemys of Egypt in the Second Century B.C., fearful that the library would surpass that of Alexandria, cut off the supply of papyrus to the scholars in Pergamon. So the scribes there turned to animals for writing materials, and the stretched skins of donkeys and sheep, treated and with the hair scraped off, came to be known

as Pergamena, or parchment in English. High-quality parchment made from the skins of calves, kids, and lambs is vellum.
—*Lutheran Digest*

Great Wall of China

If there could be creatures on Mars using telescopes to study the earth, the first evidence of life they would see is the Great Wall of China, for it is the largest thing ever built on our globe. Made of bricks nearly 2,200 years ago, it is 1,500 miles long from Kiangsu to the sea, varies from 18 to 35 feet high, and is thick enough for a road on top. It cost the lives of an estimated 400,000 workers. Many of them were buried inside the wall, which has been called "the longest cemetery in the world."—*Sunshine Magazine*

So They Say

There is an interesting story about how the military salute was started. It is said to have originated with Hannibal, the Carthaginian general. A messenger, dismounting before the great leader, was about to extend words of greeting when a fly lighted upon his nose. Because of the formality of the occasion he could hardly brush it away casually, so he snapped to attention and brushed his hand across his forehead. Hannibal interpreted this as some form of greeting and returned it. The soldiers, observing their leader's gesture, repeated it. This pleased Hannibal so much that he decided to adopt it as a form of salute, and soon it spread throughout the world.

Origin of Your Name

In early times most people bore only a first name. About the time of the Norman conquest of England, the nobility began to use the titles of their estates as surnames. The rest of the people followed the example, and assumed the names of their trades, such as Smith, Baker, Miller, Clark (Clerk), and others you will recognize among the names of your friends today.

Other names show the relationship of father and son. Wilson was originally William-his-son. Thompson and Johnson and many more were formed in this way.

The prefix O' in Ireland and Mac or Mc in Scotland has this meaning. That is, O'Hara mean the son of Hara, and Mac-Carthy means the son of Arthur. The French word for son, "fils," was corrupted into Fitz. Thus, Fitzpatrick means the son of Patrick and Fitzgerald means the son of Gerald. The Welsh indicated this same thing by the word "ap." In this way David the son of Howell was called David ap Howell, which gradually became Powell. Ap Richard became Pritchard.

As people moved from one country to another they often became known by place names. A man from Scotland would be called "the Scot," and the surname Scott would be applied to his whole family. Wallace originally indicated a person who came from Wales.

Last of the Passenger Pigeons

When Christopher Columbus discovered America in 1492, it is estimated that the number of passenger pigeons in North America was between three and five billion—not million—, and that they constituted 25 to 40 percent of the total bird population of the area that eventually was to become the United States.

This staggering number was reduced to zero in a little over four hundred years. There isn't a live passenger pigeon anywhere in the United States today.

Despite man's continuous war on them, there are many pigeons around. But they are not descendants of the wild passenger pigeon. The common domestic pigeon is a mongrelized descendant of the rock dove.

The last passenger pigeon is on display, with around 20 other birds, in a special exhibit labeled Extinction in the Museum of Natural History of the Smithsonian Institute in Washington, D.C. Her name is Martha—named for Martha Washington. She lived—that is the pigeon, not Martha Washington—in a wire cage in the Cincinnati Zoological Garden. She was exhibited as "America's last wild pigeon." Her death on September 1, 1914, marked the end of one of the most abundant bird species that the world has even known.—*Walter Hayes*

Forest Fires

In the decade that ended in 1964, there were 1,175,664 forest fires recorded in the United States—an average of 322 per day. The fires burned over more than 76,000 square miles of forest and rangeland, more than the combined areas of the states of Indiana and Ohio, taking scores of human lives and causing losses of hundreds of millions of dollars.

Why Do We Call It "Grapefruit?"

There is an interesting history back of the grapefruit which you enjoy for breakfast. Haven't you wondered sometimes why it is called "grapefruit?" It is much more like an orange or a lemon than a grape. The grapefruit does not belong to the grape family, but to the citrus family, which also contains oranges, lemons, limes, and others. Its name comes from the fact that grapefruit grows in clusters, like grapes.

This fruit is not a native of Florida, as many have supposed, nor is it a cross between an orange and a lemon, as others have claimed. The grapefruit, known as the pomola, was enjoyed in China before the time of Confucius, who lived 500 years B.C. It was first brought to Florida by a Captain Shaddock. This seafaring man had eaten the fruit in China, and was the first to grow it successfully in America.—*Sunshine Magazine*

Tip

The word "tip" comes from the letters which originally indicated the words "to insure promptness." It was the custom to hang a box on the tavern wall, into which the customer dropped a few coins to insure good service. Today, a tip seldom stands as a reward for good service, or a token of appreciation. It is expected, and is more like paying a sales tax.

Death Valley

Death Valley, in California, isn't dead! There are more than 600 varieties of plants in that vast arid region, one-third the size of Massachusetts. Fourteen varieties of birds are permanent residents, and 150 kinds are transients. The place is so hot that a wool blanket can be washed and dried in an hour —if you can find any water! The valley is hemmed in by seven mountain ranges. The lowest spot is 279.1 feet below sea level. What appears to be a desert is a fascinating place that is the home of many living things, but only those who are attuned to its beauties find that beauty in the shifting hot sands.

It's the Law!

There are still some strange laws on the books. For example: A law in Detroit regulates the size of wheat cakes. A law in Massachusetts forbids anyone to lounge on the shelves of a bakery.

A Nebraska statute forbids barbers to eat onions between 7 a.m. and 7 p.m. In Winchester, Massachusetts, a local regulation says that a young girl cannot dance on a tightrope except in church. And a law in Ohio declares that any animal on the street after dark shall prominently display a red taillight.

Way Back When—

The following rules, vintage of the 1880s, were posted in an Amboy, Illinois, store, operated by the founders of what is now called Carson Pirie Scott & Co., of Chicago:

1. Store must be open from 6 a.m. to 9 p.m. the year 'round.

2. Store must be swept; counters, shelves and showcases dusted; lamps trimmed, filled and chimneys cleaned; pens made; doors and windows opened; a pail of water and a bucket of coal brought in before breakfast. (If there is time to do so, attend to customers who call.)

3. The store must not be opened on the Sabbath unless necessary and then only for a few minutes.

4. The employee who is in the habit of smoking Spanish cigars, being shaved at the barber's, going to dances and other places of amusement will assuredly give his employer reason to be suspicious of his integrity and honesty.

5. Each employee must pay not less than $5.00 per year to the church, and must attend Sunday school regularly.

6. Men employees are given one evening a week for courting, two if they go to prayer meeting.

7. After 14 hours in the store, the leisure hours should be spent for the most part in reading.

In the 1880s, whatever else may be said, men at least learned the business, were not afraid to work, in fact were proud to work, proud to have a job, and had not learned the lesson of expecting government help.

New Year

New Year has been celebrated as a holy festival from early times. The Jews kept the Feast of Trumpets; the Druids made sacrifices, sometimes human, to their gods. In many countries gifts were exchanged on New Year, and in Scotland it used to be allowable to ask for a gift on that day. The lovely "open house" custom is English. The doors of all houses were opened at Midnight, on New Year's Eve, so that the spirit of the Old Year might go out, taking with him old habits and foolish mistakes, and the spirit of the New Year might come in with bright new resolutions.

It's Simple

This little story has been in print many times. If you tell the story to three different people, you are likely to get three different answers:

A man went into a repair shop with an impaired vacuum cleaner. He waited until the job was finished, and being told that it would cost a dollar, handed the repairman a five-dollar bill. The later was unable to make the change, so the customer said:

"I haven't another cent, and I must take the cleaner back with me. Let me have a dollar and I'll come back for the bill tomorrow."

The repairman consented, took the five-dollar bill, and handed the customer a dollar and the cleaner. The following day the man returned, gave the repairman four dollars and received his five-dollar bill back.

Was this a profitable transaction for the repairman?

Unusual Combinations

Here is a list of towns with odd names, which, with the state included, make interesting and unusual combinations:

Ash, Kan.; Oga,Ga.; Shooe, Fla.; Fiver, Tenn.; Carpet, Tex.; Odeer, Me.; Kay, O.; Skeleton, Ky. and Houdy, Miss.—*The Lookout*

The Founding Fathers

The Founding Fathers who wrote the Declaration of Independence were not, as so many think, a bunch of gray-beards. Three were in their twenties, and most of them were young. —*Ray W. Sherman*

A Mystery

For more than seventy years, the swallows which built their nests and rear their young around the historic old San

Juan Capistrano mission in Southern California have migrated southward sometime before sunrise, October 23. Their return in the spring is just as punctual, always occurring March 19. For several days before the swallows leave, a flock of "swifts," closely akin to swallows, hover around the old mission waiting to occupy the quarters vacated by the swallows. The swifts remain until the swallows return in the spring but beat a hasty retreat as soon as their cousins arrive from the South. How the swallows know the exact day and almost exact hour when they are to depart for the South or return to their summer homes is a mystery we must leave to the students of natural history.
—*Sunshine Magazine*

Sailing Westward

Contrary to common belief, the mariners in the time of Columbus generally knew that the world was round and not flat. The sailors with Columbus feared that if they continued to sail westward they would run out of supplies, not fall over the edge of the world, as some legends tell it.

100 Men

It almost seems incredible that there were less than 100 men on the three ships in Columbus' expedition. The Santa Maria had 39 men, the Pinta 26, the Nina 22.

The Dictionary

If Shakespeare had wanted to use an English dictionary he would have had to compile his own—or wait 139 years! It wasn't until 1755 that Samuel Johnson's Dictionary appeared in two large folio volumes, to become the dictionary of the English language.

Thanksgiving

Just about a hundred years ago, a certain lady in Philadelphia was quite busy writing letters to presidents, congressmen, and governors of all states. Sarah Josepha Hale was engaged in a strenuous campaign to have Thanksgiving Day become an established national holiday, to be observed throughout the country on the last Thursday in November. Sarah Hale, mother of five children and editor of a popular ladies' magazine, was the proponent of a number of new ideas and reforms. But she is best remembered, probably, for her efforts on behalf of Thanksgiving, which culminated in 1864 when President Lincoln proclaimed the national holiday.

The Costs of War

In the time of Julius Caesar, it was figured that war cost 75 cents for every killed enemy. In the Civil War, the mortality expense was $5,000 a man; in the First World War, $50,000, and in the Second World War, more than $125,000 for each casualty.
—*Sunshine Magazine*

Fancy Verse

Business is dull; can't sell a thing; the dog won't play, the canary won't sing; the radio statics, my wife has the flu; got a bill today saying, "The rent is due." Tires are all flat on the family bus; got a thousand things to make me cuss.

Yet I met a friend on the street today, who had the ungodly nerve to say: "How are you, old top? You're looking fine, without even a worry to burden your mind!".

I answered him back, strange, but it's true: "I'm fine, old fellow, how's things by you?"

This is the thought I wish to bring: The force of habit is a powerful thing!

Architecture

The first giant step toward modern architecture was taken 4,000 years ago by an ingenious Greek. He invented the "post-

and-lintel"—two columns supporting a horizontal crosspiece. Later, a clever Egyptian discovered how to take the columns away—and the arch was born. The Assyrians introduced "3-D" arches—and gave us the dome. But the Romans found that heavy domes caved in. Solution: the buttress, a super-strong support. The fifth step was taken in 1883 when William Jenney introduced the steel skeleton ("Jenney's bird cage") in Chicago—making possible the modern curtain wall.

The Good Old Days

Despite what Grandpa says, the "big family" of the "good old days" was actually less stable than the American family of today. Reason: medical progress that postpones widowhood, takes the danger out of childbirth and childhood illnesses, boosts your chances of living to see your kids grown. In 1900 the average bride and groom could expect 30 years of marriage; today's newlyweds can expect 43 years together. In 1920 one child in six was an orphan; not one child in twenty today has experienced this tragedy.

The Famous Picture "Grace"

Nearly half a century ago a photographer in Minnesota received a chance caller and the encounter brought about a world-famous photographic study.

Eric Enstrom invited the elderly peddler to dine with him and then posed him. He placed him before a small table on which was placed a large family Bible, and on it a pair of spectacles. Beside the Bible the photographer set a bowl of gruel, a loaf of bread, and a knife. Then he asked the old man to bow his head in prayer.

As soon as he had developed the negative he knew he had something special. His picture seemed to echo his words: "This man doesn't have much of earthly goods, but he has more than most people, because he has a thankful heart."

Over the years "Grace" has been hung in dining rooms and mission stations, in public restaurants and in homes throughout the world. It has become a treasured study of deep reverence, humility, and gratitude.

The Arenots

Turkish baths are not Turkish—nor are they baths; they are hot-air rooms of Roman origin.

Peanuts are not nuts; they are really beans.

The French horn is not French—nor it it a horn; it is English, and a woodwind.

The black beetle is neither black nor is it a beetle; it's another name for the cockroach, and it is brown.

The Belgian hare is not a hare; it is a rabbit.

A steel guitar is not made of steel; it is made of wood and played with a steel bar.

Westminster Abbey is not an abbey; it is the Collegiate Church of St. Peter's.

Deer's tongue is not a tongue, and has nothing in common with a deer; it is a plant whose leaves give out a vanilla-like fragrance.

Tin cans are not made of tin; they are rolled iron, thinly coated with tin.

The jugular vein is not a vein; it is an artery.

"S O S" does not stand for "Save Our Ship" as some people believe; it is simply a signal.—*Nothing But the Truth*

Good Friday

Why should we call the day of Jesus' crucifixion Good Friday? It is a designation of Anglo-Saxon background and probably originally was God's Friday. But whether God's or Good, it is a term that carries a happy connotation. On the other hand the Germanic peoples call it Karfreitag. Kar is a derivative from an old Gothic word, kara, which means black or mourning. So

Karfreitag would be Black or Grieving Friday. This more gloomy conception of Good Friday has more or less dominated the Church's observance of Good Friday down through the ages. —*Prof. Wm. E. Hulme, Wartburg Theological Seminary, "Good Friday or Black Friday?"—Pulpit Digest*

Plymouth Rock

Plymouth Rock, on which legend tells us the Pilgrims first landed, was a sizeable boulder that once cluttered up an otherwise rock-free beach. Pilgrim children may have played on and around it, but, as an old native once said, "Why any seaman would pull alongside a thing like that when he had all this fine beach, is more than I can figure. Besides, the first landing here was in a high sea that would have smashed a dory to matchwood. I figure they landed in the brook." The stone now visible is only a small part of the original, long since buried in the sand after attempts to move it resulted only in breaking off fragments. Even this sacred bit, the part souvenir hunters have left us, is shattered. Its two sections are held together by a wide band of concrete.

How's Things?

When people of various nations greet each other, here are their greetings: How do you do?—American. How do you carry yourself?—French. How do you stand?—Italian. How do you find yourself?—German. How do you fare?—Dutch. How can you? Swedish. How do you perspire?—Egyptian. How is your stomach? or, Have you eaten your rice?—Chinese. How do you have yourself?—Polish. How do you live on?—Russian. May thy shadow never be less!—Persian.

And they all mean about the same!—*Highways of Happiness*

Words

It is declared by a philologist that nine words do one fourth of our work, and an additional thirty-four serve one half of the purpose. The nine most useful words are: and, be, have, it, of, the, will, I, and you. The thirty-four that, with these nine, do half our literary work are: about, all, as, at, but, can, come, day, dear, for, get, go, hear, her, if, in, me, much, not, no, one, say, she, so, that, there, they, this, time, though, we, with, write, and your.

How It Began

In the days of Columbus, watches were unknown. To keep time aboard ship, hourglasses were used. It was the job of young boys to turn the glasses, each of which ran for half an hour, and to report to the captain that they were on the job by sounding bells. In this way, a half-hour became one bell; an hour, two bells; and four hours—the end of a watch—eight bells. The day began with eight bells for midnight, and continued in cycles of four hours each day.

Little Duplication

Of the fifty states that form the United States of America, the names of only two of them are duplicated in other parts of the world. In Russia there is a Republic of Georgia which is one of the separate units that form the Soviet Union. In France there is a region known as Maine. Nowhere in the world do we find any of the other forty-eight states' names as indicating a part of any country.

Money From Trees

People who are derided because they spend money as though it grew on trees are merely living in the wrong period of history. Money did grow on trees a few centuries ago. And people would spend it as freely as they pleased—without any wisecracks being made about it.

In the Aztec civilization as an example, the money was the tasty chocolate bean from the Cacao tree. The Aztecs had plenty of gold and silver, too, but no one was foolhardy enough to try to foist it off on the people as money. The natives knew their rights.

So a hard day's work was worth a certain number of chocolate beans. It worked out fine. There were no dangerous stock market booms and no desperate years of depression. Money crises were unheard of. And the evils of inflation were well checked. If money became too plentiful it was only necessary to practice a little crop control to decrease the cacao production. Anyone who tried black market operations was promptly and appropriately punished. Obviously the theory of plowing under the nation's wealth traces back at least as far as the Aztecs.

Often the chocolate beans were exported to neighboring nations where the purchasing natives often delightedly ate the chocolate money. This bothered the Aztecs not at all, since it gave them an opportunity to raise more money without glutting the market. As a matter of fact the life of the chocolate bean was necessarily short. It could not be very successfully hoarded, for if anyone were, for example, to bury a sock full of the monetary beans, they would soon be destroyed by rats, worms, and the elements of nature.

When their loved ones died, the Aztecs thought that they ought to take a little money with them on their journey to the next world. It might come in handy for purchasing food along the way or for bribing the guardian of the pearly gates if he attempted to deny entrance. So most of the dead were well supplied with chocolate beans. But some were supplied with beans of mud on the practical theory that a dead man could hardly tell the difference anyway.

This native shrewdness also carried over into trading practices. Like the Yankee traders who sold wooden nutmegs to unsuspecting customers, the Aztecs were not above selling canoes full of mud beans thinly overlaid with the real thing. They did a very nice business.—*The Davey Bulletin*

Such Luxury

Made of mahogany and lined with sheet metal, the first bathtub installed in the United States was installed in a Cincinnati home in 1842. It was publicly denounced as an undemocratic vanity.

Times Change

Is there something the matter with modern manners? It is said that critics today agree with one who in 1815 wrote: "What idea can the unfortunate young people of the present day have of ancient polish and refinement? So extensive is the deterioration of society, so deleterious the consequences of abandoning established systems that even the well-intentioned know not how to behave."

Perhaps the following suggestions taken from a behavior book published in 1853 will clear up a few uncertainties:

"Ladies no longer eat salt fish at a public table. The odor is now considered extremely ungenteel.

"The fashion wearing black silk mittens at breakfast is now obsolete.

"It is an affectation to eat pie with a fork and has a very awkward and inconvenient look.

"Most ladies beyond the age of thirty-five look better in caps than without them, even if their hair shows no signs of middle age."—*Sunshine Magazine*

Old Hits

A 2,300-year-old theater at Epidaurus, Greece, is still packing in audiences to watch the hit plays of 400 B.C.

After Christmas

'Twas the night before Christmas and all through the house, not a creature was stirring 'cept dad and his spouse. Their faces were haggard, all wrinkled with care. They looked at each other and sighed with despair.

Could they both be enjoying the presents they got? From the looks on their faces, we knew they were not. It was simple to us what was causing their ills. They were figuring out how to pay all those bills.

Christmas

Christmas cards made their American debut in 1875 but were acclaimed as "just another passing fad." Only a few of those early cards bore any semblance to Christmas or the winter season but, instead, stressed gay summer scenes with flowers, children, birds, and animals on display. In 1880 a Christmas card design contest was held for the purpose of "face lifting" the original designs. Rosina Emmett was winner of first prize for her painting of a group of choirboys singing, with an angel talking to a shepherd in the background. Because of the change to Christmas and winter scenes, the popularity of this Yuletide custom was here to stay.

President

Elected President of the United States by the Whigs in 1840, William Henry Harrison served one month in office—the shortest term of any American President. He was inaugurated March 4, 1941, and died April 4, exactly one month later.

Wealth

The richest man in the town of Amherst, Massachusetts, in 1772, was Nathaniel Dickinson, a Harvard graduate. He had two horses, two oxen, three cows, four swine, eight sheep, and one hundred dollars at interest. The other citizens actually were awed by all this wealth.

Calendar

Caesar revised the calendar in 46 B.C. to fit to the time elapsing each year, which is exactly 365 days, 5 hours, 48 minutes and 45.51 seconds. Inasmuch as a year is approximately 365¼ days long, Caesar decreed the fractions should be taken care of by adding a day to the calendar every fourth year. There was a slight error in his calculations and the calendar was ten days ahead of astronomical time by A.D. 1582, when Pope Gregory righted the mistake by advising the omission of Leap Year at the end of each century, except those divisible by 400. Since then our present calendar has been known as the Gregorian calendar.—*Sunshine Magazine*

True

In 1835, 1836 and 1837 the federal government was out of debt entirely.

Home

The greatest, most formidable force in the life of a child, with no second competitor, is his home. A leading Eastern University spent a quarter of a million dollars to establish this fact. This is approximately how the child's waking time is divided: The public school has him 16% of his time. The church, 1% (if he is consistent in his attendance). The home has him 83% of his time.—*Howard Hendricks, Moody Monthly*

The Versatile Clip

Paper clips are sold to clip papers together, but only about 16 percent of them serve that primary purpose, according to a study made by an English bank. They are the most versatile item in an office, for imaginative people. Approximately 20 percent are used for stakes in noon-hour card games; 5 percent do a rough job of morning manicure; 14 percent are twisted and pulled apart during phone conversations by people who can't reach a pencil and paper for doodling; 5 percent serve as toothpicks; 7 percent make emergency clothing repairs and accessories like buttons for women and tie clasps for men; 3 percent keep pipestems clear for smokers; and the rest fall on the floor to be swept away by the janitors.

Tips

We were reminded the other day that according to the best information available, the custom of tipping originated in England when small sums were dropped into a box marked T.I.P.S. —"to insure prompt service."

Cost of Land

The United States government paid 2 cents per acre for Alaska, 3½ cents per acre for the Louisiana Purchase, 27 cents per acre for the Philippines, and $294.70 per acre for the Virgin Islands.

Automobiles

We are coming to the stage when a car will be the means of traveling the shortest distance in the longest possible time. —R. A. Kidd, Time & Tide, England

A Bright Side

There is a bright side to headaches. It has been estimated that the purveyors of various headache remedies are doing some 300 million dollars' worth of business every year. In other words, every headache contributes something to the prosperity of the country.

First Air Mail?

While George Washington has been honored for many achievements as a respected citizen, a courageous soldier, a superb statesman, and a noble president, it is not too well known that he was possibly the "father of air mail." A letter signed by George Washington was believed the first carried by "air mail" in the United States. Jean Pierre Blanchard, a Frenchman, reportedly carried the letter in a balloon flight from a Philadelphia prison yard to Woodbury, New Jersey. The flight was fourteen miles long; the date, January 9, 1793.

How to Ride a Bicycle

With bicycle riding becoming more and more a family hobby, parents will want to instruct their children properly. These directions are quoted from a magazine published in 1891:

"The pedal should be pressed downward, not with the heel of the instep, but with the toes and the ball of the foot, thus giving the ankle free play and producing the full development of the calf muscles of which the good rider is justly proud. In mounting the bicycle the gentleman has the left pedal up and slightly in advance of center. Placing the left foot upon it, and clasping the handlebars, he throws his weight upon the left foot, swings the right leg easily over the wheel and settles into the saddle. In dismounting he checks the motion by letting the pedal on the upstroke lift his weight; at the same time his right leg describes a graceful arc above the rear wheel and comes to rest on the ground at the left.

"A lady must, of course, mount in different fashion. Stepping through the drop frame and making sure that her skirts are nicely draped around her ankles on either side, she lifts herself into the saddle by pushing down on the left pedal, in the same effort starting the bicycle in motion."

The Zero Hex

The last seven men elected to the Presidency of the United States, in a year ending with a zero, died in office. Four of them were assassinated and three of them died natural deaths:

William H. Harrison, elected in 1840, died in 1841.

Abraham Lincoln, elected in 1860, was assassinated in 1865.

James A. Garfield, elected in 1880, was assassinated in 1881.

William McKinley, elected in 1900, was assassinated in 1901.

Warren G. Harding, elected in 1920, died in 1923.

Franklin D. Roosevelt, elected in 1940 (third term), died in 1945.

John F. Kennedy, elected in 1960, was assassinated in 1963.

The only other president to die in office was Zachary Taylor, who was elected in 1848 and died in 1850—a year with a zero in it.

They Serve a Purpose

Rows of tiny stiff bristles on the body of an earthworm are the means by which it travels. The attempt of a robin to pull an earthworm from its burrow is made difficult by the extending of these bristles into the walls of the burrow.

The Flag

The first flag of the United States was the Grand or Great Union Flag which was raised on Prospect Hill in Somerville, Massachusetts, by George Washington's Continental soldiers on New Year's Day in 1776. The following year, Congress created our flag, which had 13 stars and 13 stripes, representing the 13 colonies. When Francis Scott Key saw the flag waving triumphantly over Fort McHenry in 1814, and was inspired to write The Star-Spangled Banner, it had 15 stars and 15 stripes. More stars and stripes were added for each new state, until 1820, when Congress decided the National Flag would have 13 stripes, and a new star would be added with the admission of each new state.

Dog Chaser

One of the first automobile accessories featured by Packard in 1902 was a gun that squirted ammonia about eight feet. Its purpose was to discourage dogs from chasing cars and taking nips at the tires which, in those days, were so thin and moved so slowly that they were always in danger of being punctured by playful canines.

CHAPTER 5

PERTINENT STORIES AND OBSERVATIONS

Blind

Bernard Baruch wrote, "I have known men who could see through the motivations of others with the skill of a clairvoyant, only to prove blind to their own mistakes. I have been one of those men."

Language

A long time ago, a Chinese sage was asked by his pupils what he would do first if he had the power to set right the affairs of the country. He answered: "I should certainly see to it that language is used correctly." The pupils look puzzled. "Surely," they said, "this is a smaller matter. Why do you say it is so important?" And the wise man replied: "If language is not used correctly, then what is said is not what is meant; if what is said is not what is meant, then what ought to be done remains undone; if this remains undone, morals and art will be corrupted; if morals and art are corrupted, justice will go astray, the people will stand about in helpless confusion."—*Adult Leadership*

We Mass-Produce Almost Everything—
EXCEPT CHARACTER

It used to be that, when you wanted something, you worked to earn it. Now you stage a riot to get it given to you at someone else's expense.

If your father or grandfather lost his job, he took whatever work he could get, and he went (probably walked miles) to where there was work—only honest work—being done. Now hordes of relief "clients" refuse a job unless it is to their liking, and they demand the job be brought to them in their community.

This nation was built by immigrants (beginning in the 1600s and earlier) who struggled here for opportunity, and would have scorned the false idea of "something for nothing." Now it seems to be an almost universal (and all too often, the only) ambition.

It used to take a lifetime of gruelling work and scrimping for a family or a country to earn a little surplus, a taste of security. Now mobs of stupid "students" and whole "emerging nations" demand they be given it, out of your earnings and with no effort on their part.

"Minority groups" all over the earth seem to think the world owes them everything they want. So vicious destructiveness makes necessary higher taxes for playgrounds; higher taxes for schooling for gangs who don't seem to want or are unable to be educated. The minority groups whose rights no one seems to consider are the taxpayers and decent citizens—who may have been pampering evil too long.—*From an advertisement of Warner and Swasey*

It's Easy—Until

It's easy to sit in the sunshine
And talk to the man in the shade;
It's easy to sit in a well-made boat
And tell others just where to wade;
It's easy to tell the toiler how

Best to carry his pack,
But you never know the weight of the load
Until the pack is on your back.—*The Lutheran Digest*

Money

Workers earn it, spendthrifts burn it, bankers lend it, women spend it, forgers fake it, taxes take it, dying leaves it, heirs receive it, thrifty save it, misers crave it, robbers sieve it, rich increase it, gamblers loose it—we could use it.

—Richard Armour

The Barefoot Boy

Blessings on thee, little man, barefoot boy with cheeks of tan! Trudging down a dusty lane with no thought of future pain; you're our one and only bet to absorb the national debt. Little man, with cares so few, we've a lot of faith in you, guard each merry whistled tune, you are apt to need it soon. Have your fun now while you can; you may be a barefoot man!

Conscience

Conscience is that still small voice that quells a wicked thought, then adds this warning sequence, "Besides, you might get caught."

Age

An unfailing sign that age creeps on apace is when you say, "Your father was a great friend of mine," and learn you should have said grandfather.

The Difference

The difference between a "wise guy" and a wise man is plenty.

Conscience is a still small voice that makes you feel still smaller.

Perhaps

Perhaps Korea was the end of the road for classical armed aggression against one's next-door neighbor; perhaps Suez was the end of the road for colonial-type military solutions; and perhaps Cuba was the end of the road for nuclear confrontation.
—*Adlai E. Stevenson*

Right-Hand Door

Why do folks who look quite sane treat life and limb with such disdain, by looking neither left nor right when they from motor cars alight, but step into the traffic stream from left-hand doors, loudly scream when drivers, skidding to a stop, ask them if they have blown their top!

I almost fear, 'most any day, I'll catch some idiot that way, and leave him dead, sans all palavar, a very badly spoiled cadaver.

So brother drivers, I implore, please get out the right-hand door!

Education

The day after the circus came to town, a teacher of the first grade received the following excuse for the absence of one of her pupils:

"Dear Teacher: Education, you know, is a lot of things. It is reading and writing and ciphering. It is 'yes, please' and 'yes, thanks,' and 'no, thank you.' It is the washing of our hands and the use of forks. It is pencils and scissors and paste and erasers and chalk dust. It is the smell of a school room early Monday morning. It is the excitement of vacations. It is autumn bonfires and sleds and puddle-wading.

"Yes, education is a lot of things. It is a brass band blaring and a calliope tooting. Education is a woman shot from a cannon, a man on a tight rope, a seal playing a tune with his nose. It is sideshow barkers, clowns, lions, cotton candy, cowboys and spangles. Education is the wonderment of new things and new sensations. It is, in short, a circus!

"That's why Ginger wasn't in your classroom yesterday. Excuse it, please."

How It Started

The word, "handkerchief," shows to what extremes we sometimes go in the English language. "Kerchief," from the French couvre-chef, means covering for the head. To this the English added "hand," meaning a covering for the head held in the hand. When we say "pocket handkerchief," we are really saying a covering for the head which is held in the hand which is contained in the pocket.

Bluff

Clyde Beatty had little trouble controlling a cageful of jungle cats with two things—fearlessness and an ordinary kitchen chair. No animals should be afraid of a chair but they are. Beatty found them like human beings, largely bluff. We humans often act like those animals, allowing ourselves to be bluffed by something that has little or no reality. When we are afraid to tackle some task, let us ask ourselves, "Are we being bluffed by a kitchen chair?"

Then You Are Older

You are no longer as young as you used to be when you suddenly discover that it takes you longer to rest than it does to get tired.

A Moral

Mary had a little cold, but wouldn't stay at home, and everywhere that Mary went, the cold was sure to roam.

It wandered into Molly's eyes and filled them full of tears; it jumped from there to Bobby's nose, and thence to Jimmie's ears. It painted Anna's throat bright red, and swelled poor Jennie's head; Dora had a fever, and a cough put Jack to bed.

The moral of this little tale is very quickly said—Mary could have saved a lot of pain with just one day in bed!

The Men Started It

Do you complain about the hours your wife spends at the beauty parlor? If so, you might be interested in the fact that you have your male forebears—to blame.

All the things milady finds so necessary for beauty were originally invented for, and used by, men. Historians say men were the first to curl their hair, put on cosmetics, don silk stockings—and even wear high heels.

The dandy of yesteryear was a gay bird, to be sure. On the other hand, such frills were forbidden for women; their garb was dull by comparison.

The Road is Always Better

"The road is always better than the inn." These words by the great Spanish writer, Cervantes, mean a way of living. In my younger days I often aimed too hard to reach some goal, finish some job. "When this is done," I'd say, "I shall find real satisfaction and reward." But later I came to realize that each achievement, like each inn, is only a point along the road. The real goodness of living comes with the journey itself, with the striving and desire to keep moving. Now I find that I can look back on my 84 years with pleasure and, what is even more important to me, that I can still look to the future with hope and desire. I have learned to take each inn along the way with a traveler's stride—not as a stopping point, but a starting point for some new and better endeavor.—*Maurice Maeterlinck*

Worrying

Sir Winston Churchill's prescription against worrying: "When you feel vaguely oppressed write down all the things that you can think of as possible annoyances: 'This one doesn't mature for six months. I know the answer to this. This is the only real difficulty that is crying for an answer.' Then you deal with it. For you make it all manageable the moment you break it up into precise and concrete issues. The thing that the human mind can't stand up against is mystery."

Great Moments

Our greatest moments have been those in which our faith overcame tragedy. The Pilgrims at Plymouth Rock, Captain John Smith and his devoted band of early settlers at Jamestown, Washington at Valley Forge, Lincoln on his knees at the White House—these were our greatest hours. Out of these hours God brought forth America.

Not Probable

An atheist confronted a scientist and expounded his views that God did not create the world. To which the scientist replied, "The probability of life originating from accident is comparable to the probability of the dictionary resulting from an explosion in a printing shop."

The Twenty-One Gun Salute

One signer of the Declaration of Independence, Francis Hopkinson of New Jersey, was a notorious doodler. After his death a story was written about his doodling. Hopkinson, late in 1776, was toying with the year, "1776," a famous one in American history. He finally came up with the idea of adding the figures across and found they came to twenty-one. He then said to himself, "Why not a twenty-one gun salute for the Presidents?" He submitted his idea to members of Congress who liked and approved it. It has been in use ever since.

Civilizations

Historian Arnold Toynbee in Moody Monthly said: "Of the twenty-two civilizations that appear in history, nineteen of them have collapsed when they reached the moral state the United States is in now."—*Sunshine Magazine*

From a Little Acorn

In 1913, the tax on a $4,000 income was a penny.

Old Expressions

The word "Selah" appears in the Bible 74 times, yet it has never been defined and no one knows what it means. The following expressions are contained in the Bible: "There is nothing new under the sun." "A man after his own heart." "Eat, drink, and be merry." "Apple of his eye."

It Was a Good Story

Nero did not play a "fiddle" or any other instrument at the burning of Rome, according to Tacitus, the historian. The "fiddle" was not yet invented, and Nero was fifty miles away, and did not return to the city until it was in ashes.

Modern Youth

The child of olden days walked a couple of miles to and from school, made his own amusement devices, thought a penny a fortune, went barefoot in summer, wore knee pants until he was old enough to work, and was certain of only three days of the week: Friday, Saturday and Sunday. Friday was the last day of school, Saturday he took his weekly bath, and Sunday he put on his best and went to church. His modern counterpart is driven two blocks to school, has ready-made toys, thinks pennies are good only in parking meters, owns shoes for all occasions, gets long pants as soon as he can walk, and is a human calendar as far as knowing which day of the week it is. How? By TV programs.

Swedish Proverbs

No one has so big a house that he does not need a good neighbor.

Guests should not forget to go home.

He who buys what he doesn't need steals from himself.

Don't throw away the old bucket until you know whether the new one holds water.

Being young is a fault which improves daily.

A life without love, a year without summer.

Better to suffer for the truth than be rewarded for a lie.

Business

The American business man has a problem; if he comes up with something new the Russians invent it six months later and the Japanese make it cheaper.

Our Duties and Our Rights

Our task as Americans is to strive for social and industrial justice, achieved through the genuine rule of the people. This is our end, our aim, our purpose. The methods for achieving the end are merely expedients, to be finally accepted or rejected according as actual experiences show that they work well or ill.

The leader for the time being, whoever he may be, is but an instrument to be used until broken, and then to be cast aside; and if he is worth his salt, he will care no more when he is broken than a soldier cares when he is sent where his life is forfeit in order that the victory may be won. In the long fight for righteousness, the watchword for all of us is give and be given. It is of little matter whether any one man fails or succeeds; the cause shall not fail, for it is the cause of mankind.

220

We must insist that there shall be self-control on the part of the people, that they must perceive their duties as well as their rights, that they must be jealous of the rights of others as of their own.—*Theodore Roosevelt, 26th President of the United States (1858-1919)*

Problems

A true philosopher has opined that most of life's problems are really like those cloverleaf exchanges on our highways: It may not seem like it at first, but there's always a way out.

Federal Aid

Federal aid is like giving yourself a blood transfusion by drawing blood from your right arm, returning it to the left arm, and spilling more than half of it on the way across.—*Joseph Kilgore*

Christmas

When the landlord wants the rent of your humble tenement; when the Christmas bills begin daily, hourly, pouring in; when you pay your gas and light rate, tip the rector, fee the curate, let this thought your spirit cheer: Christmas comes but once a year.

When you roam from shop to shop, seeking till you nearly drop, Christmas cards and small donations for the rest of your relations, questing vainly 'mid the heap for a thing that's nice, and cheap: Think, and check the rising tear, Christmas comes but once a year.

When mince pies you can't digest, and all the foods you love the best, join their forces in a fight to keep you stirring all the night, and then next day you really should be in a gay, convivial mood—bear with fortitude and patience these afflicting dispensations: Man was born to suffer here; remember—Christmas comes but once a year!

What Is It All About?

James Truslow Adams, the American historian, wrote this: "Perhaps it would be a good idea, fantastic as it sounds, to muffle every telephone, halt every motor and stop all activity some day to give people a chance to ponder for a few minutes on what it is all about, why they are living, and what they really want."

The Long, Wrong Road to Peace

When Pyrrhus was about to sail for Italy, Cineas, a wise and good man, asked him what were his intentions and expectations.

"To conquer Rome," said Pyrrhus.

"And what will you do next, my Lord?"

"Next I will conquer Italy."

"And after that?"

"We will subdue Carthage, Macedonia, all Africa and all Greece."

"And when we have conquered all we can, what shall we do?"

"Do? Why, then we will sit down and spend our time in peace and comfort."

"Ah, my lord," said the wise Cineas, "what prevents our being in peace and comfort now?"

Opportunities to "Do Good"

Too many of us get it into our heads that to "do good" we must go far outside our daily routine interests.

Glenn Frank once said: "The rich man's greatest opportunity for public service lies inside his private business. That is to say, statesmanship in business is of greater social value than philanthropy outside business."

A man with the genius for successfully running a business is right where he belongs; the opportunities to "do good" are greater in business than outside business.—*William Feather*

Stars Too

The Netherlands flag is red, white and blue, too. So a Dutchman told an American friend, "Our flag has a connection with taxes," he explained. "We get red when we talk about them, white when we get our tax bill and we pay them till we're blue in the face." The American exclaimed, "That's just how it is in the United States, only we see stars, too!"

Money

Money will buy a bed, but not sleep; books, but not brains; food, but not appetite; finery, but not beauty; a house, but not a home; medicine, but not health; luxuries, but not culture; amusements, but not happiness; religion, but not salvation.

I Agree

When creditors growl and almost bite,
I find I must agree:
I couldn't sleep a wink at night,
If I was owin' me!—*Howard Bradley Smith*

Wisdom

The trouble with people these days is that they want to reach the promised land without going through the wilderness.

Contented Cows

We've known about synthetic silk, but now they've made synthetic milk! To me it seems a thing demented—and I hope the chemicals are contented!

Middle Age

I used to think that middle age would make me witty, wise, and sage; but now that I have reached the spot, I'm not those things that I was not.

Gets It Quicker

All things come to him who waits; but here's a rule that's slicker: The man who goes for what he wants will get it all the quicker.

Dissenter

The dissenter is every human being at those moments of his life when he resigns momentarily from the herd and thinks for himself.—*Archibald MacLeish*

Knowledge

In the business world an executive knows something about everything, a technician knows everything about something, and a switchboard operator knows everything.

Traffic Sign 1975

Northbound traffic keep to right around cloud.

Getting Older

A sure sign you're getting older is when the kids come home from school and tell you about their history lessons and you realize that when you went to school the same items were called "current events."

The Duties of a Bank Director

"There ain't nuthin' to it. You go into the fancy meeting room and you just sit there and never open your yap. As long as you don't say nuthin' they don't know whether you're smart or dumb. When the question of a loan comes up if it's a friend of yours you vote to give it to him and if he ain't a friend you don't."—*Casey Stengel, manager, New York Mets, and director of a Glendale, California bank, as told to Arthur Daley of the New York Times.*

Test Your Spelling

To test the spelling ability of anyone, dictate and have him write the following series of sentences. If fewer than eight errors are made, the person can be rated as an excellent speller. If more than twenty are misspelled, he is just an ordinary word-bungler:

An irreligious peddler and an embarrassed cobbler were harassed by bulletins charging that they kidnaped a bottle of asafoetida to inoculate some picnicking acquaintances against catarrh.

"Your innuendo is sacrilegious," spieled the peddler, fingering a woolly queue which he used to camouflage his spherical skull.

"I saw the thief, a traveler in the cemetery, reveling in the symmetry of the obelisks."

His alibi seemed impregnable enough to supesede legal procedure; so the sheriff recommended that the bailiff release him.

"This plaguy, desiccated, and rarefied air will give him a hemorrhage anyway," he said.—*Sunshine Magazine*

Modern Youth

A father was reading some nursery rhymes to his young son.

When he read the line, "The cow jumped over the moon," the boy stopped him and said, "They must have fed the wrong figures into the computer or the tracking center didn't correct his position. He had too much thrust for his load. Obviously the systems were not all go-go and the radar must have been out of order or he wouldn't have missed the moon by that far."

Patience Exhausted

Representative Sidney R. Yates says he was always impressed by the ability of the interpreters while he was a member to the United States mission to the United Nations.

"But I recall one translation that occurred at the end of a day-long debate.

"An impassioned delegate cried, 'Will we never be rid of armaments?' The weary interpreter—and I will always believe he did it deliberately—translated it:

" 'Will we never be rid of arguments?' "

Busy

Here lies a poor woman who always was busy; she lived under pressure that rendered her dizzy. She belonged to ten clubs and read Browning at sight, shone at luncheons and was out every night. She served on committees, and went near and far; she golfed and she "kodaked" and drove her own car.

Her children she saw only once in a while; her husband signed checks and tried hard to smile. One day on her schedule, she found an hour free; the shock was too great, and she died instantly.—*Sunshine Magazine*

You Wouldn't Know the Old Place Now

Arizona Progress in a recent and rather morose survey of housing trends laments that the Old Homestead has shrunk from a three-story labyrinth of halls and compartments to a functional one room igloo resembling a space ship that has been converted into a drive-in hamburger stand. There are no longer rooms, merely "living areas." The article continues: "The bathroom is the only area with a door that closes—but we have the uneasy feeling that this relic of Victorianism will not long survive. The garden is full of furniture and the house is full of plants. This is somewhat confusing to the birds and bees although it simplifies matters for the flies and ants."

A Short Story

One day a young man found a $5.00 bill between the ties of a railroad. From that time on he never lifted his eyes from the ground while walking. In 30 years he accumulated 25,916 buttons, 62,172 pins, 7 pennies, a bent back, and a sour, miserly disposition. In "finding all this, he lost the smiles of his friends, the songs of the birds, the beauties of nature, and the opportunity to serve his fellow man and spread happiness."—*From Kitchener's Shepherd's Staff*

Just Try It

A wise man never plants more than his wife can hoe.

Modern Isms

Several economists have recently attempted to vitalize their platitudes — and embellish their abstractions — by describing various "Isms" in terms of two cows. Inasmuch as this is a game that anyone can play, we give you herewith a few homespun definitions.

Capitalism: If you have two cows, you sell one and buy a bull. Your herd increases in size, value and productivity.

Socialism: If you have two cows, the Government takes both of them and gives you back a little skim milk. This is known as redistribution of wealth.

Communism: If you have two cows, the Government shoots you, gives the cows to your neighbors and issues a manifesto to the effect that milk is a poisonous secretion produced only by capitalistic mammals.

Government Plan: If you have two cows, the Government shoots the bull—and then milks the taxpayer.

Realism: If you have two cows, both of them are dry.

Rugged Individualism: If you have two old cows that have gone dry, you sell them to another rugged individualist at twice the value—and then criticize the Government because you must pay a tax on the profit.

Marxism: If you have two cows, you are a capitalist.

—*Arizona Progress*

So They Say

By the time the youngest children have learned to keep the place tidy, the oldest grandchildren are on hand to tear it to pieces again.—*Christopher Morley*

Life is made up of sobs, sniffles, and smiles—with sniffles predominating.— *O Henry*

The best medicine I know for rheumatism is to thank the Lord it ain't gout.—*Josh Billings*

Pessimism, when you get used to it, is just as agreeable as optimism.—*Arnold Bennett*

He wasn't exactly hostile to the facts, but he was apathetic about them.—*Wolcott Gibbs*

I've got a lot of books but no bookshelves; but then nobody lends bookshelves.—*W. Victor Smethurst*

Think of what would happen in America if there were no humorists; life would be one long Congressional Record.

—Tom Masson

Advice

You should have quit when you were behind.

—James B. Reston

Life Begins

When a man wakes up to the fact that his span of life is shortening with every clock tick, and if he is going to live a useful life he must be at it—at that moment life begins for him no matter what his age. The tragedies of life are with those who never discover that life has begun.

For them the curtain never rises.

Congressional English

Justice Felix Frankfurter (dissenting, 1959) said in a Supreme Court case dealing with a taxpayer's duty to file a declaration of estimated income tax:

"If Congress chooses by appropriate means for expressing its purpose to use language with an unlikely and even odd meaning, it is not for this court to frustrate its purpose. The court's task is to construe not English, but congressional English. Our problem is not what do ordinary English words mean, but what did Congress mean them to mean."—*Commissioner vs. Acker, 4 L.Ed. 2nd. 127*

The Great and Noble

Where you are is of no moment, but only what you are doing there. It is not the place that ennobles you, but you the place; and this only by doing what is great and noble.—*Petrarch*

Cut It Short

A certain South African tribe has one custom that might well be introduced in this country. Considering long speeches injurious to the orator and to the audience as well, they have an unwritten law that a public speaker must stand on one foot while addressing his listeners. As soon as the other foot touches the ground, the speech is brought to a close—by force if necessary!

Correct

It was a wise youngster who, on being asked, "What is the chief end of man?" replied, "The end that's got the head on."

Saving and Spending

Spending what should be prudently saved, or saving what should be prudently spent, are both wrong.—*Owen D. Young*

Hardship

Pity the poor high school kids. Lots of them have to walk nearly as far to their parked cars as we used to walk to school. —*Memphis Commercial Appeal*

No One Greater

From the Talmud, foremost work of post-Biblical Jewish literature, comes this version of the story of Adam: "One man alone was brought forth at creation in order that no man may say to another, 'My father was greater than your father.'"

Confucius No Say

Men who leave home to set the world on fire, often come back for more matches.

When man works like horse, everybody rides him.

Little sugar plums today sometimes sour grapes tomorrow.

Man can read some people like book but can't shut them so easily.

Coat of paint sometimes make old house look like new, but not old woman.

Breath of scandal makes breezy conversation.—*The Rounds*

The Guy in the Glass

When you get what you want
In your struggle for pelf,
And the world makes you King for a day,
Then go to a mirror and look at yourself,
And see what that guy has to say.

For it isn't your Father, or Mother, or Wife
Who judgment upon you must pass,
The fellow whose verdict counts most in your life
Is the one staring back from the glass.

He's the fellow to please, never mind all the rest,
For he's with you clear up to the end,
And you've passed your most difficult, dangerous test.
If the guy in the glass is your friend.

You may be like Jack Horner and chisel a plum
And think you're a wonderful guy,
But the man in the glass says you're only a bum,
If you can't look him straight in the eye.

You can fool the whole world down the pathway of years,
And get pats on the back as you pass,
But your final reward will be heartache and tears,
If you've cheated the guy in the glass.

—Anonymous, Worden & Risberg

I Didn't Have a Very Happy Childhood, Either . . .

But nobody worried very much about it. I was too busy, I guess—cutting lawns, shoveling snow, running errands, delivering packages for ten cents, selling newspapers, doing housecleaning for my mother, and going to school. I passed my grades, too; if I hadn't I'd have had the hide strapped off me.

No one concerned himself about my amusements, either. What fun we had, we made. But if we did any damage like breaking a window in a ball game, we paid for it by working it out.

We never heard these modern phrases like "standard of living," "subsistence level," "minimum requirements." Our standard of living was whatever my father (and after I was about 12, my father and I) earned. I don't suppose people "understood" me and if I had said so, my mother would have asked, "Why should they?" And certainly no one ever gave a thought to my "problems." They were mine, weren't they? Mine to solve. Why should I expect anyone else to bother?

If my father were laid off, we stopped spending on anything but food, and a lot less of that. My dad spent every waking hour looking for work—any work. We lived on savings and when they were gone, we moved in with relatives. If there had been no relatives, when every penny and every salable asset was gone, we would have gone to the only place left—the County Poor House—but that would have been an admission that we couldn't take care of ourselves.

You'll notice in this true story of a typical American family of a few years back, I'm not talking about privileges nor happiness. I guess we didn't have much. But we had something that was infinitely more important, infinitely more rewarding—we had self-respect, because whatever we had, however little it was, we earned.

It seems to me that is why America is the strong nation it is today—and it will stay strong only as long as there are enough Americans more interested in earning than getting.

—Advertisement of Warner Swazey of Cleveland, Ohio

He Works Hard

The average American is a man who works hard all winter to fill his home with comforts and conveniences, and then spends his summer in a trailer, fishing boat, or mountain shack with few comforts and conveniences.

Names

If status can be achieved by adopting a high-sounding name, the scavenger service should be near the top that hung on one of its garbage trucks this sign: "Used Vitamin Convoy Service."

Ministers

A schoolboy in an Anglican school was asked to write a note on the clergy. Here was his effort: "There are three kinds of clergymen—bishops, wreckers and curates. The bishops tell the wreckers to work and the curates do the work. A curate is a thin married man, but when he becomes a wrecker he gets fuller and can preach longer sermons, and becomes a good man."

—Church Management

Lessons From a Dog

Here are a few things you can learn from your dog:
To keep clean.
To love children.
To keep your place.
To size up an enemy.
To drink plenty of water,
To be a dependable friend.
To express pleasure when favored.
To guard faithfully the interests of those who care for and protect you.
To be faithful unto death.

If a Child Lives

Why do some youngsters grow up to be well-adjusted adults, while others go wrong? There is no simple answer to this question, but most psychologists agree that children are inclined to follow the example set by their parents. With this thought in mind, perhaps, an unknown writer created this list of cause-effect observations:

If a child lives with hostility, he learns to fight.

If a child lives with criticism, he learns to condemn.

If a child lives with fear, he learns to be apprehensive.

If a child lives with jealousy, he learns to hate.

If a child lives with self-pity he learns to be sorry for himself.

If a child lives with encouragement, he learns self-confidence and integrity.

If a child lives with praise, he learns to be appreciative.

If a child lives with acceptance, he learns to love.

If a child lives with approval, he learns to like himself.

If a child lives with fairness, he learns justice.

If a child lives with honesty, he learns what truth is.

If a child lives with friendliness, he learns that the world is a nice place in which to live.—*Sunshine Magazine*

Small World?

We hear a lot now about how small the world has grown. It has grown small only in terms of time and distance. It has grown tremendously big and complicated in terms of its problems and the way these problems can be solved. If we must have a strong government to lead us through this difficult period, I think we must have strong businesses to support that government, businesses with the ability to carry their share of the national burden.—*John Dykstra*

We Know

We used to think we knew we knew, but now we must confess, the more we know we know we know, we know we know the less.

The Intellectual Approach

The University of Louisville began using the intellectual approach to persuade students not to walk on the grass of the beautifully kept lawn. Two large, attractively lettered signs were erected on the campus at strategic points, saying:

"To the art student: We appeal to your sense of beauty.

"To the math student: The shortest distance between two points is not a straight line—here.

"To the science student: Cynodon dactylon (Bermuda grass) is not indestructible.

"To the psychology student: We appeal to your inner emotions.

"To the music student: Like man—yeah. Walks are to walk on."

At the bottom of the signs is a more traditional phrase: "Please keep off the grass!"

Computers

Don't underestimate the power of automation and the electronic computer. A computer demonstrator in New York City, for example, has explained that "it would take 50 men working day and night for 200 years to make the same mistake that this machine could make in only two seconds!"—*Railway Clerk*

Conformity

We try to be like others, to conform, so that we will be accepted. But only to the degree that one is different has he anything to offer. Every contribution is an evidence of difference, of uniqueness.—*Don Robinson*

Achievement

Louis A. Miazza, a certified public accountant of Jackson, Mississippi, tells of an executive who has a plaque on which one lone word appears: A P E. People who see the plaque are curious. This executive explains his capsule wisdom. Each of the three letters of the word APE stand for a word. The three words are. Analyze, Plan, Execute. The executive explains that if we do these three things we are likely to succeed in our life's endeavors. All we have to do is APE them!—*Rotator (Macomb, Illinois)*

Books

Good books are good friends, the wisest and wittiest nearly all of us can hope to meet, and I never put one down without a feeling of quiet exultation that I have been lifted out of myself and am a better person because of it: more informed, more perceptive and understanding, more articulate, and thus able to contribute more to my family, friends, and society.

—George Waller

School Superintendents

Some wag has described the life of a (school) superintendent in the following manner: The first year you are eulogized. The second year you are criticized. The third year you are ostracized. The fourth year you get fired. There may be more truth than poetry in this statement, because the average tenure of school administrators in the U. S. is approximately four years.—*Earle W. Wiltse, Education Digest*

Birthstones

For laundresses, the Soapstone.
For architects, the Cornerstone.
For cooks, the Puddingstone.
For politicians, the Blarneystone.
For borrowers, the Touchstone.
For policemen, the Pavingstone.
For stockbrokers, the Curbstone.
For shoemakers, the Cobblestone.
For burglars, the Keystone.
For tourists, the Yellowstone.
For beauties, the Peachstone.
For editors, the Grindstone.
For motorists, the Milestone.
And still another might be added!
For careless drivers, the Tombstone!

Eyes Ahead

You're flirting with death when you hail a friend; keep your eyes on the road or your friendship may end.

Time Marches On

Mary had a little watch; she swallowed it—it's gone. Now everytime that Mary walks, time marches on!

Hard Luck

Joe saw the train but didn't stop. They dragged his flivver to the shop. It only took a week or two to make the car as good as new; but though they hunted high and low, they found no extra parts for Joe.

The Fickle Public

An author wrote a little book which started quite a quarrel; the folks who read it frowned on it and said it was immoral.

They bade him write a book of worth. He said that he would try it. He did. With it they found no fault—but neither did they buy it.

Harem Scarem

A Sultan at odds with his Harem, thought of a way he could scare 'em; he caught him a mouse, which he freed in the house, thus starting the first Harem Scarem.

Changed View

He shouted of the curse of wealth and made the rich man wince. But an uncle left him money—and he hasn't shouted since!

Fishing

There are two reasons for the proverbial persistence of anglers. The first is that the fish are biting; the second is that they are not. Either is a sufficient justification for fishing a little longer.—*Fred Steever, Forbes Magazine*

Early Surly Bird

Cheerful people, the doctors say, resist disease better than the glum ones. In other words, it's the surly bird that catches the germ.

Rules for Brains

If every automobile driver would use his brains, show reasonable courtesy to other drivers, and exercise his common sense, there would be no need for traffic rules. But we have to have traffic rules because rules have to be used when brains aren't.

Satisfied

From the top of a hill an old Indian showed his son the valley below with its blue lake, luxuriant woods, and broad, fertile fields. Then he said, "Hope palefaces do go to the moon. Indians be plenty satisfied just to have this."

Modern Sayings

All that too many of our modern people remember of Patrick Henry's famous saying is "Give me . . . " and even that is distorted into the modern "Gimme!"

If you want to be original, be yourself. God never made two people exactly alike.

Men show their characters in nothing more than in what they think laughable.

When a man says he can get on without religion, it merely means he has a kind of religion he can get on without.—*Harry Emerson Fosdick*

To a Five-Dollar Bill

Crinkle, crinkle, little bill; goodness, gracious, you look ill! Are you losing all your power? You seem weaker hour by hour.

"Now that prices are so high, I'm so tired that I could die. I just circulate all day, no one dares put me away. When the evening board is set with the fruits of father's sweat, my small voice is hushed and still—I am in the butcher's till. And no matter where I go, people disregard me so; I don't seem to count for much 'mongst the profiteers and such."

Bill, take heart, your luck may change. I'll admit the times are strange. Though you're weak I love you still—crinkle, crinkle, little bill.

(This poem was first published in 1919!)—*Sunshine Magazine*

They Can't Fire Her

I don't have to say that "my grandmother died" if I want to turn out for the Giants; my boss won't grumble, my boss won't chide; I've sure got it down to a science.

I don't have to faint or resort to tears or use any feminine wiles. They can't fire me—for the past two years I've been keeping the office files.

I've got the names of the firm's officials neatly arranged by their middle initials. Customers' letters I've filed instead by the color and size of their letterhead.

I've put Mrs. Duffy's damage suit in a folder entitled "Big Dispute"; and for anything I consider extraneous, I've three whole drawers marked "Miscellaneous."

Oh, they can't fire me if I don't come at all; they've got to take it smiling. I've got them backed up against the wall for I do all the filing.

He Knew His Business

There's nothing quite so charming as the rows of waving corn where farmers do their farming on a hot midsummer morn. No sound is quite so thrilling as the whistling that is done through constant hours of tilling, underneath a boiling sun. No job is quite so earthy as the pushing of a plow, and nothing seems so worthy as the tending of a cow. No picture is as pretty as a farmer mowing hay.

My home is in the city. That's where I plan to stay.

Knowledge On Trees

How nice 'twould be if knowledge grew on bushes as the berries do; then we would plant our spelling seed, and gather all the words we need! And sums from off our slates we'd wipe and wait for figures to be ripe, and go into the field and pick whole bushels of arithmetic!

Or, if we wished to learn Chinese, we'd just go out and shake the trees, and grammar, then, in all our towns would grow with proper verbs and nouns; and in the garden there would be great bunches of geography; and all the passersby would stop and marvel at the knowledge crop!

That's Different

The joke you just told isn't funny one bit. It is pointless and dull, wholly lacking in wit. It's so old and so stale it's be-beginning to smell. (Besides, it's the one I was planning to tell.)

Open Road

I think that I shall never see a billboard lovely as a tree. Indeed, unless the billboards fall I'll never see a tree at all.

The Mendacity of Specificity

With a touch of cynicism, Professor Cyril N. Parkinson has stated certain now famous economic laws, one of which is that government expenditures always rise to meet government income. No matter how much revenue a government receives, a way is found to spend it.

Dr. John K. Langum, an economist, says he has a law for describing those who make forecasts on the business outlook. He thinks his law is fully as significant to mankind as Professor Parkinson's law on government expenditures. Dr. Langum's law states that "the higher the index of specificity, the higher the coefficient of mendacity." In other words, "the more specific a person is in forecasting the business outlook, the more he deceives you."

Humility

North Carolina is a valley of humility between two peaks of conceit.—*Former U. S. Senator A. Willis Robertson*

Silence

There is no sound so terrible to an actor as silence.—*Ethel Barrymore*

Toys

When it comes to Christmas toys,
Time turns back, and men are boys.

Dedication

Our need in this day is a series of specific, precisely-defined objectives beyond ourselves, to which we will devote ourselves as a people and undertake whatever sacrifices may be required.
—*Dr. Robert F. Oxnam*

Work

Work is everybody's birthright. To youth it brings hope; to middle-age, confidence; and to the aged, repose.
—*Eugene P. Bertin, Pennsylvania School Journal*

Knowledge

Etc. is a sign used to make believe you know more than you do.

Training and Experience

Training means learning the rules. Experience means learning the exceptions.

Common Sense

One pound of learning requires ten pounds of common sense to apply it.—*Persian proverb*

Teacher

A teacher is a person helping a child to grow, to mature and to become a man.—*Leo R. Ward, Philosophy of Education*

Foreign Aid

Commented an official in the foreign-aid program: "There are four things every 'new nation' seems to want: A steel mill, a national airline, an eight-lane highway and a chance to make a speech before the National Press Club in Washington.—*U. S. News & World Report*

What to Tell a Son

If I had a son, I believe I could help him most by providing him with these five indispensables: A personal example to follow, an understanding of the importance of restraint and ideals, a sense of discipline, a pride in his heritage, and a challenge to meet.—*J. Edgar Hoover, Christian Science Monitor*

Details

A speck cuts the value of a diamond in half—a race horse that can run a mile a few seconds faster than any other is worth twice as much. That little extra all through life proves to be the greatest value.—*John D. Hess, Arizona Architect*

City

A city is an organization of human beings, a living thing, and its character depends wholly upon the people who compose it, who built it, shaped it, own it and live in it. It is progressive or backward, beautiful or ugly, orderly or slovenly, well managed or inefficient, growing or gradually dying, all depending upon the spirit, intelligence, aims and ambitions and moral character of its citizens.—*W. H. Bartholomew, Architect*

Responsibility

If you want your father to take care of you, that's paternalism.

242

If you want your mother to take care of you, that's maternalism.

If you want the government to take care of you, that's socialism.

If you want your comrades to take care of you, that's communism.

But—if you want to take care of yourself, that's Americanism!

Christmas

We trim the tree on Christmas night, and trim the house with holly bright. But poor old Dad—he gets trimmed first, and what is more, gets trimmed the worst. But, still, he never says a word; so here's to Dad—a game old bird!

Economist

An economist is a Ph.D who will give you a dim view of the obvious for a fee.

Race Relations

Race conflict is irrational because it is irrelevant to what is distinctively human in our human nature. . . . Our human spiritual life is what is distinctive and important in us; and for human beings to quarrel over their spiritual differences does therefore perhaps make some sense, though it is deplorable that we should misbehave toward each other on any grounds at all. But to quarrel over the minor external physical differences between one breed of Homo sapiens and another! This is a form of criminal insanity that is confined to human adults.—*Arnold J. Toynbee, New York Times Magazine*

Old-Fashioned

Sixty years ago folks boiled coffee and settled it with an egg. The only reds known were red flannels, and a boy didn't think he had to have a vehicle in which to pursue happiness. People were more interested in the contentment of each other than they were in cows.

Ladies rode sidesaddle, and when the preacher said a truth the people said, "Amen." A candidate had to be economy-minded to get elected to office.

Neighbors asked about your family and meant it. And when a man dressed for the evening he put on his nightshirt. Folks used toothpicks, and were still polite.

Two or three people could meet without passing the hat. Parents were the only baby-sitters.

And men knew that the reward of idleness was hunger and want, not an unemployment compensation check; and that their future security depended on what they saved today, not what their children and their children's children would pay in taxes, ad infinitum.—*Sunshine Magazine*

Books

An evening spent reading great books does for our minds what a holiday in the mountains does for our bodies. We come down from these lofty heights stronger, our lungs and our minds cleansed of all impurities, and we are better equipped to face with courage the battles on the plains of daily life.

—Andre Maurois

So Rich - So Poor

It is a curious fact that a nation so rich in science should be poor in international relations, that a nation so advanced in medicine should be so poor in theology, that a nation so expert in advertising should be so inept in the study of ideas.

—Charles T. Thrift Jr.

Boners

In Christianity a man can have only one wife. This is called monotony.

The greatest miracle in the Bible is when Joshua told his son to stand still and he obeyed him.

Heredity means if your grandfather didn't have any children, then your father probably wouldn't have had any, and neither would you, probably.

Power

There have been very few individuals in the history of the world who could be trusted with complete, unadulterated, omnipotent power over their fellow men.—*Justice Hugo L. Black*

Color

June is a riot of color. Fields turn green. Brides dress in shimmering white. Graduates sport tassles of gold. And the government ends another fiscal year in the red.

—U. S. Senator Norris Cotton

Behavior

Good behavior gets a lot of credit that really belongs to lack of opportunity.—*Reveille, London*

Wisdom

To remind a man of the good turns you have done him is very much like a reproach.—*Demosthenes*

Advice is like snow; the softer it falls, the longer it dwells upon, and the deeper it sinks into, the mind.

—Samuel T. Coleridge

Thinking is the talking of the soul within itself.—*Plato*
The truth never hurts—unless it ought to.—*B. C. Forbes*

Memory

A good memory is a very nice thing to have, but a perfect memory—absolutely and unqualifiedly perfect—God forbid: It would crowd our minds like an office where nothing ever gets thrown out, neither third class mail nor fifth class nor junk.
—*Alexander Gode, Journal of the American Medical Association*

As They'd Say It Today

Jonah—"You can't keep a good man down."

Samson—"I'm strong for you."

David—"The bigger they are, the harder they fall."

Helen of Troy—"So this is Paris?"

Nero—"Keep the home fires burning."

Noah—"It floats."

Methuselah—"The first hundred years are the hardest."

Columbus—"I don't know where I'm going, but I'm on my way."

Elizabeth to Sir Walter Raleigh—"Keep your shirt on."

Sir Walter to Elizabeth—"Step on it, Liz."

Peace

Two very famous artists were asked to paint pictures that would express their idea of peace. One painted a beautiful lake surrounded with colorful flowers and shrubs, behind which on gently rolling pasture lands grazed contented cattle. The other artist painted a waterfall plunging to the rocks below making a fine spray as it hit the bottom where it roared and tumbled tumultuously. On a ledge of rock behind the seething cataracts the artist painted a little mother bird quietly sitting on her nest.—*Uplift*

No Criminals

Sunday schools do not make criminals. This is my observation across 72 years of life. If a criminal is found in a community where there are Sunday schools it is almost always a certainty that he hasn't been a regular attender of any. Judges who have looked into the crimes of any country find that almost all of the criminals come from a class of people who are not brought up in Sunday school or church.

—*Walter E. Isenhour, Wesleyan Methodist*

Importance of Names

An aged criminal lawyer explains how he was always able to cheat the gallows for his clients: "I never say 'my client' or 'the defendant'; I always say 'Tom Jones' or 'Henry Brown.' Juries will hang clients and defendants, but they haven't the heart to hang Tom Jones or Henry Brown."—*The Pilot*

Parental Authority

Sally and James Reston seem to be speaking from experience when they confess: "Helping your eldest son pick a college is one of the great educational experiences of life—for the parents. Next to trying to pick his bride, it is the best way to learn that your authority, if not entirely gone, is slipping fast."

—*Sunshine Magazine*

You Can't Win

The boss must gauge his movements by some queer quirk of fate; he comes at noon when you're on time and early when you're late!

Use of Words

There's always a different way of saying something that may not sound so good, unless you rephrase it. Instead of "They repossessed my car," why not say, "My balance sheet shows a reshuffling of proprietary interests." Or instead of "I lost my Japanese camera," just explain, "I've disposed of a segment of my foreign holdings." Figure one out for yourself and try it on your friends.

Listen for the Knock

Some unknown fabulist told the tale of how the Wolf and Opportunity met at the door of a humble cottage. The one knocked and the other howled. Behind the door lived an Optimist, full of hope. He was expecting Opportunity and heard the knock but not the howl. And then the two, the wolf and Opportunity, went to another door. The one howled and the other knocked. Behind this door lived a Pessimist, full of despair. He was expecting the Wolf and heard the howl, but not the knock.

High-Toned Talk

One of the bright boys in the Bureau of Statistics sent out a market report. He was trying to say that prices would continue to rise. This is the way he said it: "Within a short segment of time there will undoubtedly be witnessed the continuing definite inception of an upward tendency unless unfavorable contingencies which are at present unpredictable create cross -currents in the national economy."

These Are Bad—Can You Do Better?

If the red rooster had the toothache, would the leghorn pullet?

If the golf balls, will the tree leave?

If the yeast foams, why can't the cream puff?

What will honeydew when she finds she cantaloupe?

If the mulberry leaves, will the banana split?

If the chocolate drops, will the wristwatch the eggbeater?

If a ham hangs in the smokehouse, where will the veal loaf?

If the bedspread, will the pillow slip?

Will the lipstick, if the earrings?

Did Tennessee all that Arkansas?

Will the corn get shocked if it sees the barn dance?

Automobiles

More and more people have two cars in their garage, neither one paid for. I can remember back when a family took a Sunday drive they all got in one car.—*Red Blanchard, Wallace's Farmer & Iowa Homestead*

Probably Right

When the U. S. detonated its night high-altitude shot over the Pacific Ocean, the sky was lit up for hundreds of miles by the man-made sun. For example, it was bright enough for a news photographer to take a long-range photograph of Diamond Head, the craggy peak that has become something of a trademark for the Hawaiian Islands. In Samoa, a reporter of the *New York Times* explained to a horrified native what had caused the night sky suddenly to lose its darkness. The native became pensive. The reporter asked if he had any comment. The native nodded, and then pronounced the most succinct judgment of the event, and perhaps of the age, yet recorded. "White man is crazy," he said.—*Norman Cousins, Saturday Review*

It Makes a Difference

If I park carelessly with my car, what difference does it make?

If I don't thank a person for a job well done—especially when he goes out of his way to help me—what difference does it make?

If I don't acknowledge someone when he opens the door for me, what difference does it make?

Stop and think of the difference it can make:

Careless parking—using 1½ stalls instead of one—eliminates up to 50 parking places in each of our lots every day. Second Shift employees often must go to another lot to find a place to park.

249

If you don't express appreciation to a person for extra effort on a job, it doesn't take long for his enthusiasm to dampen, and his cooperation to slack off.

Even when you fail to heed someone opening a door for you or—if you're a woman—to acknowledge the traditional respect gentlemen grant ladies, you have ignored a basic factor in getting along with others.

What are we talking about?

Courtesy, of course. It's the go-power behind most human teamwork and cooperation. It works wonders.—*Caterpillar Folks*

Is It Possible?

There is considerable question about our methods of education in the minds of many intelligent persons today. Is it possible that we are not teaching our sons to think, to be independent men? Are we becoming soft—seeking comfort and security more than we seek freedom? It was on this road to comfort and security that the free citizens of Athens—who had the first democracy, and the greatest democracy in the world until ours—lost their freedom, their democratic form of government, and themselves.—*American Appraisal Company*

The American Society

"Ladies and gentlemen," the pilot said, "I have two pieces of news for you. One of them is good and one of them is not so good. So I'll tell you the bad news first. The bad news is that we are lost; we don't know where we are. But as I told you, there's good news, too. The good news is that we have a 200-mile-an-hour tail wind."

There are times when it seems to me that that story sums up the current state of American society; we don't know where we are going, but, quite clearly, we are getting there awfully fast. One of the most dramatic manifestations of this is the vast difference in attitudes between the current crop of young people and their parents—that painful lack of communication which the press has christened "the generation gap."—*David Rockefeller*

Patriotism

Patriotism is a lively sense of collective responsibility, an expansion of filial love, a kind of religion. . . . True love of country is not mere blind partisanship. It is regard for the people of one's country, a feeling of fellowship for them, and a desire for their prosperity and happiness.—*Eugene P. Bertin, Pennsylvania School Journal*

Education

The job of the school is to educate the child, not to bring him up.—*Dr. Arthur Larson*

Industry

After a great deal of experience and observation, I have become convinced that industry is a better horse to ride than genius. It may never carry any man as far as genius has carried individuals, but industry—patient, steady intelligent industry—will carry thousands into comfort, and even celebrity. —*Walter Lippman*

A Lesson in Hebrew

The following is taken from "The Bible Speaks to You," by Robert M. Brown:

The Hebrew alphabet had no vowels and no punctuation. What is more, all the letters were run together. If you wrote that way in English, you would have something like this:

MTHLRÐYRGDWHBRGHTYTFTHLNDFGYPT
TFTHHSFBNDGYSHLLHVNTHRGDSBFRM

If you can guess where the vowels go and what they are, and how to divide the words thus found, you can finally figure

out that this sentence reads: "I am the Lord your God, who brought you out of the land of Egypt, out of the house of bondage. You shall have no other Gods before me." (Exod. 20:2, 3)
—*Sunshine Magazine*

Courtesy

Courtesy is really nothing more than a form of friendliness. It is amazing what a warming influence it can have on an otherwise dreary world. It has been said that a rise of one degree Fahrenheit in the mean annual temperature of the globe would free both polar regions from their ice. It is thrilling to contemplate what frigidity might be dispelled in the world of human relations if people made just a little better effort to be friendly.
—*Rotagraph (Ft. Worth, Texas, Rotary Club)*

Trouble

Never attempt to bear more than one kind of trouble at once. Some people bear three kinds: All they have had, all they have now and all they expect to have.

Ignorance

An ignorant adult is more dangerous than an ignorant child because the ignorance level of the adult rises as his knowledge gap grows wider and wider.—*Wilber V. Bell*

Fatigue

A medical school professor once told me, "Never ask a patient whether he is tired." "Why not?" I asked. "Because everybody is tired. This symptom is worthless in diagnosis."
—*J. DeWitt Fox, M.D.*

Books

There is only one recipe for a best seller and it is a very simple one. You have to get the reader to turn over the page.
—*Ian Fleming, Chicago Tribune*

CHAPTER **6**

QUICK QUIPS

More boners are pulled on school exams than there are jokes on television. Read these answers:

"William Tell invented the telephone."

"Two occupations of the civilized race are work and looking for work."

"In mathematics, Persia gave us the dismal system."

"Chemistry is the study of how a thing that is busted gets together under certain situations, and how them that's together gets separated."

"A circle is a round line with no kinks in it, joined up so as not to show where it began."

"To keep milk from turning sour, keep it in the cow."

"Universal suffrage was when the whole world suffered."

"Savages are people who don't know what wrong is until missionaries show them."

An antique is something no one would be seen with if there were more of them, but which everyone wants when no one has any."—*Chatham Blanketeer*

Golf liars have one advantage over the fishing kind—they don't have to show anything to prove it.—*Bing Crosby*

It's easy to be beautiful—just be born that way.

—Suzy Parker

If a woman is an hour late in returning home, and her husband is worried, she is flattered. If a man is three hours late, he is angry if anyone is worried.—*Johnny Carson*

Members of the younger generation are alike in many disrespects.

Polygamy would never work in this country. Think of six wives in a kitchenette.

The woman whose husband weareth not the scarf she knitteth him may be said to have cast her purls before swine.

Nothing seems to make a man as eager to get ahead in the world as a long line of cars ahead of him.

Most people don't believe they are having a good time unless they are doing something they can't afford.

People are like tea bags. They don't know their own strength until they get into hot water.

A pessimist is a guy who crosses his fingers when he says, "Good Morning."

A husband is a guy who has taken up spousekeeping.

A diplomat is a man who puts his best foot forward when he doesn't have a leg to stand on.

Our problems are all alike, except that I don't worry about yours.

Pessimist—One who has the discouragement of his convictions.

Antique show—Late movie on TV.

Panhandler—A housewife.

An executive is a man who goes from his air-conditioned office in an air-conditioned car to his air-conditioned club to take a steam bath.

Practicing physician—a doctor who says, "If this doesn't cure you, I'll give you something that will."

Orator—A man who can take a 300-word idea and blow it up to hold six thousand more.

A garden plot—The bugs and worms planning to eat up your garden stuff.

Taxation—The art of so picking the goose as to secure the greatest amount of feathers with the least amount of squawking.

Modern music—The kind that puts the "din" in dinner and takes the "rest" out of restaurant.

Literary aspirant—What an author takes when he has a headache.

Cooperation—A word consisting of eleven letters that can be spelled with two—W-E.

Inflation is when after you get your salary it isn't enough.

Lawyer—Shrewdest distance between two points.

Economist—One who is uncertain about the future and hazy about the present.

I'm a guy who has spent his life shoving a camera down the throat of history.—*David Douglas Duncan*

Love is an ocean of emotions, entirely surrounded by expenses.—*Lord Dewar*

Maybe the magazines one finds in the dentist's waiting-room are put there to indicate how long the dentist has been practicing.

A man who thinks he is more intelligent than his wife is married to a smart woman.

Women are made to be loved, not to be understood.

—Oscar Wilde

A tax cut is the kindest cut of all.

I enjoy TV commercials. It's nice to see something on television you know won't be interrupted.

My wife has a very magnetic personality. Everything she lays her hands on she charges.

Taxi driver—Person who runs into so many interesting people.

Money—It may talk but it never seems to hear us calling for it.

Modern furniture—Furniture that becomes antique before it's paid for.

Extremist—A man who gets his shoes shined and his hair cut at the same time.

Lobster-Newburg—A dish ordered in restaurants by those who usually get hamburger at home.

Dime novel—A book which has gone up—to three dollars.

Desire—The thing that is so often nipped in the budget.

Forest fires—Caused by tourists—when they're through with the scenery, they burn it.

Etiquette is knowing which finger to put in your mouth when you whistle for the waiter.

The only trouble with some of these fine homes is their location—on the outskirts of our income.

It seems that every year it takes less time to fly across the ocean and longer to drive to work.

Don't throw away your empty seed packages. They are often just the right size for storing your crop.

Another man who can never find things where he puts them is the amateur gardener.

Boy—A noise with dirt on it.

A little monkey grows up to be a big monkey; a little pig grows up to be a big pig, and man, wonderful man, can grow up to be either.

People will believe anything if you whisper it.

"Doctors are only human," says a medical journal. Yes, they like to talk about their operations.

In olden times the building of a new house involved a public ceremony known as raising the ridgepole. Today it involves a private ceremony known as raising the money.

Many a person is dominated by a rich uncle's will power.

The head of a leading university says he is trying to develop a school the football team can be proud of.

It used to be that a fool and his money were soon parted, but now it happens to everybody.

Sign in optometrist's window: "If you don't see what you want, you've come to the right place."

When a pessimist thinks he's taking a chance, the optimist feels he grasping a great opportunity.

A sweater is a garment a child wears when his mother feels chilly.

Marriage would work out better if both sides would operate on a thrifty-thrifty basis.

Weddings have become so costly that it's now the father of the bride who breaks down and weeps.

When a kid misbehaved 50 years ago to get attention, he really got it.

Why can't life's problems hit us when we're eighteen and know all the answers?

What the country really needs today is a credit card that will fit in a vending machine.

An orator is one who makes loud noises from the throat sound like deep messages from the brain.

Speaking of tranquilizers, even back in Grandpa's time, there was something to make you sleep. They called it work.

The American way—Using instant coffee to dawdle away an hour.

If you think twice before you speak, you'll never get into the conversation.

At age twenty we don't care what the world thinks of us; at age fifty we find out it wasn't thinking of us at all.

People come in three classes: the few who make things happen, the many who watch things happen, and the overwhelming majority who have no idea what happened.

Moonlighter—A man who holds day and night jobs so he can drive from one to the other in a better car.

If the kids are running the country, we wish they'd set the grown-ups a little better example.

Nice thing about drive-in movies is that you know where your wife's shoes are when you want to go home.

Some kids think a pioneer family is one that moved to the country before it became a suburb.

A problem child is one who puts two and two together and gets curious.

Plastic surgeons can do almost anything with a woman's nose except keep it out of other people's business.

Washington analysis of a top foreign diplomat—He is one who knows how to refuse American aid without managing to be deprived of it.

A good scare is worth more to a man than good advice.

His first bill from the country club sometimes makes a new member wonder if he was accepted . . . or taken.

Average father—One who wears out a pair of shoes while the rest of the family wears out a set of tires.

Modern version—Don't put off until tomorrow what you can do at overtime rates today.

You can take a day off, but you can't put it back.

Don't worry when you stumble; remember a worm is about the only thing that can't fall down.

It's too bad more people are thoughtless than speechless.

Flattery is the art of telling another person exactly what he thinks of himself.

The trouble with being a good sport is that you have to lose to prove it.

Always do right. This will gratify some people and astonish the rest.—*Mark Twain*

What this country needs is tranquility without tranquilizers.

Putting off an easy thing makes it difficult; putting off a hard one makes it impossible.

Sometimes you can judge a man by the company that keeps him.

They say that love makes a girl nine feet tall. So does a trip to the hairdresser.

Prince Philip at Institute of Personnel Management in London: "The trouble with British industry is that there are too many one-ulcer men holding down two-ulcer men's jobs."

"It's not that I really cheat," the golfer explained, "it's just that I play for my health, and the low score makes me feel better."

Middle age—When you have that morning-after feeling without the night before.

When you are down and out, something always turns up—and it is usually the noses of your friends.—*Orson Wells*

In these days of two-car families, about the only thing that can keep a family together is being unable to get one started.

The small boy who voluntarily washes behind his ears is probably looking for his gum.

Modesty—The feeling that others will discover how wonderful you are.

Even though they haven't a leg to stand on rumors have a way of getting around.

Don't tell the tired-looking person that he needs a vacation; the chances are he just had one.

A lot of fellows who complain about their boss being stupid would be out of a job if the boss was any smarter.

Too much of the world is run on the theory that you don't need road manners if you drive a five-ton truck.

American diplomacy is easy on the brain but hell on the feet.—*Charles G. Dawes*

Restaurant sign: "Customers who find the waiters rude should see the manager."

He who laughs last—has an insecure upper plate.

In this season of decision, the world is watching America. America is watching television.

Truth has to change hands only a few times to become fiction.

Snobbery is the luxury of the fool.

No man is a successful liar unless someone believes him. —*Dun's Review*

A secret many find hard to keep is their opinion of themselves.

Learn to say "No!" It will be of more use to you than to be able to read Latin.—*Charles H. Spurgeon*

If you can't find it in the dictionary, the atlas, or encyclopedia, don't be discouraged; ask for it at the drug store.

If you want to know what your wife is going to ask you to do next, try sitting down.

If the family budget looks sick at the end of the month, it's probably something you ate.

A hobby is an endless amount of hard work that you would be ashamed to do for a living.

The home may lose popularity, but there never will be a substitute place to eat corn-on-the-cob.

Love of money is the root of half the evil in the world, and lack of money, the root of the other half.

Too many hosts seem to think that the best way to open a conversation is with a corkscrew.

Definition of a desk: a waste basket with drawers.

Fish seem to grow faster during the first few weeks after they are caught.

He who hesitates is honked at.

There are some friends you can depend upon—always around when they need you.

The newest dream kitchen has a lounge with TV, book-cases, and fireplace, but most women would chuck the whole thing for a good, old-fashioned hired girl.

Poise is the ability to be ill at ease naturally.

You may be able to make some people think you are younger than you are, but you can't fool a hamburger sand-wich just before bedtime.

It's always easier to arrive at a firm conviction about a problem after you know what the boss thinks.

Any government that is big enough to give you everything you want is big enough to take everything you have got.

Before the craze for split-level homes a fellow kept it to himself if he lived over a garage.

Even when a marriage is made in Heaven, the maintenance work has to be done here on earth.

Parking space: An unoccupied area along the curbing on the other side of the street.

Congress is confronted with the unsolved problem of how to get the people to pay taxes they can't afford for services they don't really need.

Generosity is giving away what you could use yourself. —*Marianne Moore*

Life can be understood only backward, but it must be lived forward.—*Soren Kierkegaard*

Our future as a nation is going to depend not so much on what happens in outer space as on what happens in inner space —the space between the ears and in the soul.—*Alfred Arens*

I wish I were either intelligent enough to understand our present tax and fiscal policies or stupid enough not to worry about them.—*Representative John W. Byrnes*

Some never think of what they say; others never say what they think and both are as boring as those who always say what they think.—*Joel Brown*

These days, a man's life depends not so much on the star under which he was born as the color of the light, when he crosses the street.

There can be little doubt that we have made tremendous progress in medicine during the last generation. What used to be merely an itch is now an allergy.—*Grit*

An economist says we must have an "elastic currency." He should say adhesive.

It is a dull man who is always sure, and the sure man is always dull.—*Henry L. Mencken*

Take the humbug out of this world, and you haven't much to do business with.—*H. W. Shaw*

The dictionary is the only place where success comes before work.

A conservative is one who acts impulsively after thinking a long time.

Winter is the time of year when children leave open the doors they slam shut in the summer.

Nature did not make us perfect, but it has compensated us by making us blind to our own faults.

If you don't enjoy what you have, how would you be happier with more?

Ignorance: The beauty of it all is, it won't cost a cent; we'll get it all out of tax money.

Living the past has one thing in its favor—it's cheaper.

Men who try to do something and fail are much better off than those who try to do nothing and succeed.—*R. W. Emerson*

If you think old soldiers just fade away, try getting into your old army uniform.

Prosperity is what keeps us in debt.

No man is so full of wisdom that he has to use his mouth as a safety valve.

One of life's unsolved mysteries: Why, when you are "lying awake all night," does the clock strike only the half hours so that you never know what time it is?

The optimist always wants you to cheer up when things are going his way.

The boss: "to no him is to get fired."

If you want to see a baseball game in the worst way, take your wife with you.

A clear white skin is a girl's best friend—especially if it's ermine.

He was the type of guy who'd turn out to be a stool pigeon in the choir.—*Fred Allen*

Common sense gets a lot of credit that belongs to cold feet. —*Arthur Godfrey*

A real TV fan is a guy who thinks that dining out means eating in the kitchen instead of the living room.

An egotist is usually me-deep in conversation.

One of my chief regrets during my years in the theater is that I couldn't sit in the audience and watch me.

—*John Barrymore*

It's all right to talk to yourself as long as you don't listen. —*Barbara Nichols*

I know a fellow who was born with a silver spoon in his mouth. He hasn't stirred since.

An auction is a place "where you get something for nodding."

Give me my golf clubs, the fresh air, and a beautiful girl for a partner, and you can keep my clubs and the fresh air.
—*Jack Benny*

If at first you don't succeed, try, try a couple of times more. Then quit. There's no sense in making a fool of yourself.

—*W. C. Fields*

I never forget a face—but in your case I'll make an exception.—*Groucho Marx*

What used to be television station breaks are now better defined as compound fractures.

A straw vote only shows which way the hot air blows.
—*O. Henry*

Every married man should forget his mistakes in life. There is no sense in two people remembering the same thing.

—*Sam Cowling*

I had just enough white man's blood in me to make my honesty questionable . . . In the early days of Indian territory there were no such things as birth certificates. You being there was certificate enough . . . Once you are a showman you are plumb ruined for doing manual labor again . . . I've never seen a mayor who wasn't funny—and when he puts on a silk hat he's even funnier. What this country needs is more ex-mayors.
—*Will Rogers*

A woman will not be the first human to land on the moon. She couldn't decide what to wear.

The ultimate consumer—the worm.

Thoughtless person—one who is also seldom quiet.

Profanity is the effort of a feeble mind to express itself forcibly.

A liar is one who has no partition between his imagination and his information.

Courtroom—A place where justice is often dispensed—with.

Nothing maddens a politician so much as the discovery that the other side is playing politics.

Then there was the bell ringer who got tangled in the rope and tolled himself off.

There are so many laborsaving devices on the market today that a man has to work all his life to pay for them.

If an automobile dealer drives a car five hundred miles, it is nicely broken in; if we drive it fifty miles, it is a used car.

The leader of the orchestra is always a man who has played second fiddle.

The moon sways the tide, and also the untied.

Charm is a woman's strength, while strength is a man's charm.

Heredity is something people believe in if they have a bright child.

The average taxpayer is the first of America's natural resources to be exhausted.

A real friend is a fellow who doesn't mind bothering you.

You never hear of anyone giving the groom a shower. They figure he is all washed up anyway.

Preacher—One who always has eloquence on tap.

It may be a man's world, but chances are it's in his wife's name.

A proverb is a short sentence based on long experience.

If you think twice before you speak, you'll never get into the conversation.

It takes a hunk of remembering to remember back when charity was a virtue, not an industry.

Wrinkle—The nick of time.

Another reason why you can't take it with you—it goes before you do.

Sometimes it takes a lot of scratching to get out of a situation you were just itching to get into.

Traffic at rush hours is often at a standstill.

The dime isn't really worthless. It still makes a fairly good screwdriver.

Speak when you're angry and you'll make the best speech you will ever regret.

If you feel that you have no faults—that makes another one.

There's nothing else in the world like a hard day's work —and aren't you glad there isn't?

A budget is a contraption that shows how much you are going to have to borrow.

He who laughs last probably wanted to tell the story himself.

The reason most people know little about what's going on in the world is that this information isn't in the comic strips.

A man hopes that his lean years are behind him; a woman, that hers are ahead.

Where did you get the idea that swimming is good for the figure? Did you ever take a good look at a whale?

Only a woman can skin a wolf and get a mink.

Most people can keep a secret; it's the folks they tell it to who can't.

An American can consider himself a success when it costs him more to support his government than to support his family.

If at first you succeed, you probably haven't accomplished very much.

Adolescence is the period when children are certain they will never be as stupid as their parents.

Listening to advice may get you into trouble, but it makes the other person feel better.

Golf is no longer a rich man's game. There are millions of poor players.

There are times when if you are not feeling like yourself, it is quite an improvement.

Pawnbroker: One who lives off the flat of the land.

Conscience is a still, small voice that tells when you are about to get caught.

Time was when men lost their shirts in the stock market; nowadays it's in the supermarket.

In the last analysis ability is commonly found to consist mainly in a high degree of solemnity.—*Ambrose Bierce*

Running into debt isn't so bad. It's running into creditors that hurts.

A deficit is what you have when you don't have as much as if you had nothing.

A model wife is one who, when she spades the garden, picks up the fish worms and saves them for her husband.

A bore is somebody who goes on talking while you're interrupting.

Faster and more frequent mail service seems desirable until you see what you are getting.

A person has to work himself to death to buy all those labor-saving devices these days.

What the elephant said to the maharajah: "You may be on top now, but wait till we come to a long hanging branch."

If you're gonna be a sneak at least be open and above board about it.

A taxi driver is one guy who thinks nothing of going out of his way to make a dollar.

Awkward age: Too old for the peace corps, and too young for social security.

Exhibitionist: Any girl with a new engagement ring.

Mechanic wanted. Honest appearance a must.

Double jeopardy: When your doctor calls a consulting physician.

Repartee: Sophisticated insult.

Opinion: Prejudice with a few unrelated facts.

Success: When you have your name in everything but the telephone directory.

He was no yes man. When they said no, he said no, too.

A parent was so rich he didn't know he was putting his son through the university.

If you feel neglected, think of Whistler's father.

The worst thing about retirement is having to drink coffee on your own time.

An inventor is a crackpot until he hits the jackpot.

You're getting old when the gleam in your eye is from the sun hitting your bifocals.

I have an appointment with my psychiatrist and if I don't get there on time he goes right on without me.

Voice out of the woods, "Never mind the golf ball, caddie, come and find me."

Sign in a Pentagon office: Look alive. Remember you can be replaced by a button.

The best way for a housewife to get a few minutes to herself at the end of the day is to start doing the dishes.

I have been called a charlatan and a genius. It's possible both statements may be true.—*Pablo Picasso*

An adolescent is a minor who is a major problem.

One research typist to another, "Between Unplanned Parenthood and Planned Obsolescence there'll always be work for us advertising people."

Summer picnics would be a great invention—if they could work the bugs out.

Persons hardest to convince they are of retirement age are children at bedtime.

An adolescent is a teen-ager who acts like a child when she's not treated like an adult.

Women's styles may change but their designs remain the same.—*Oscar Wilde*

Somerset Maugham: At a dinner party we should eat wisely but not too well, and talk well but not too wisely.

Mark Twain: Always do right. This will gratify some people and astonish the rest.

Middle age is when you start out with your spirits up and end with a rubdown.

To be a gentleman is a worthy trait, but it is a great handicap in an argument.

We all like to give people the benefit of our experience, but we should know they won't take it because everyone wants to see for himself if the paint is wet.

Statistics indicate that the average family could use more money than it is getting—and usually does.

There are people who roll out the carpet for you one day—and pull it out from under you the next.

Doing housework for so much a week is domestic service, but doing it for nothing is matrimony.

We'd better protect the birds. The dove brings peace, and the stork brings tax exemptions.

Prosperity is that wonderful time when you can always get enough credit to live beyond your means.

A woman's ideal man is one clever enough to make money and foolish enough to spend it.

Oh, for the good old days of normalcy—when everybody made five dollars a day and spent ten!

A smart girl is one who knows how to play golf, tennis, the piano, and dumb.

Inflation: Prosperity on the cuff.

An income is the sum of money it costs you more to live than.

A pessimist is a person who absorbs sunshine and radiates gloom.

Although unpaid bills are by no means rare, they are nevertheless considered collectors' items.

Marriage teaches you loyalty, tolerance, understanding, perserverance and a lot of other things you wouldn't need if you'd stayed single.

The easiest way to stay awake during an after-dinner speech is to deliver it.

A smart aleck is a fellow who thinks he knows as much as you know you do.

One of life's briefest moments is the time between reading the sign on the freeway and realizing you just missed the off-ramp.

Money can't buy love, but it certainly makes shopping for it very interesting!

The things money can't buy are wonderful, but the things money can buy aren't bad.

Self-control might be defined as the ability to carry a credit card and not abuse it.

The best way to serve spinach and parsnips is to someone else.

An extravagance is anything you buy that is of no earthly use to your wife.

Every man should have a fair-sized cemetery in which to bury the faults of his friends.—*Henry Ward Beecher*

If you must borrow, borrow from a pessimist. He won't expect it back.

You're getting old when the doctor who is giving you a checkup is younger than you are.—*Red Skelton*

Why, with all that land in the western movies, are the heroes always in the path of the stampede?

Today's progressive American is one who wears last year's suit, drives this year's car, and lives on next year's salary.

You will always stay young if you live honestly, eat slowly, sleep sufficiently, work industriously, worship faithfully—and lie about your age.

Money used to talk; now it just sneaks off when no one is looking.

Civilization is a system under which a man pays a quarter to park his car so he won't be fined a dollar while spending a dime for a nickel cup of coffee.

The easiest way for a man to get his wife's attention is by looking comfortable.

Christmas holidays: Anticipation, preparation, recreation, prostration, and recuperation.

It is sad to see people squandering money and know you can't help them.

It's great to have your children home from school. It takes your mind off your other troubles.

It's a wise child who resembles a wealthy relative.

Regardless of what the Supreme court says, there will be prayers in our schools as long as there are exams.

Many people fail to recognize opportunity because its favorite disguise is hard work.

A bird sanctuary is a tweet land of liberty.

I'm sorry that some of you have to stand for this talk; and I include those who are seated.—*Bishop Fulton Sheen*

Remember way back when all you could get on the cuff was gravy?

Tourists are so thick they were getting into each other's snapshots.

An alarm clock is a mechanical device to wake up people who have no children.

Before retiring take a week off and watch day-time television.

Man is the only animal who goes to sleep when he isn't sleepy and gets up when he is.

The only thing children wear out faster than clothes is parents and teachers.—*Kiel Record*

If at first you don't succeed, you're about average.

—*Joan Nelson*

The best way to remember your wife's birthday is to forget it just once.

Some politicians think profits are wicked, but they certainly meet the payroll better than deficits.

The most courteous tax collector in the country is the filling station man who also sells gas and oil as a sideline.

Grandma may have worked harder as a housewife, but she never had to clean out the swimming pool.

Years make all of us old and very few of us wise.

Everyone has one thing he can do better than anybody else, and usually it's reading his own handwriting.

If you want to know how long it will take to get to the top, consult a calendar; if you want to know how long it takes to fall to the bottom, try a stop watch.

Some doctors tell their patients the worst—others mail the bill.

If the grass is greener on the other side of the fence, you can also bet the water bill is higher.

He who hesitates misses picking up the dinner check.

At a certain time in every man's life he suddenly realizes that the human race is run over a very short course.

You know it's time to resume your diet when even your safety belt gets too tight.

Many a wife has helped her husband to the top of the ladder —then left him there while she decided where else the picture would look good.

It's easy enough to be grouchy, when things aren't coming your way, but the prize old growl is the man who can howl when everything's going O.K.

Baldness: Man's oldest fallout problem.

We spared the rod and got a beat generation anyway.

A psychiatrast says conceit is a form of illness. It's a strange ailment that exhilarates the victim and makes his associates sick.

A born leader sees which way the crowd is going and steps in ahead.

Social security: The system that guarantees you steak when you have no teeth with which to chew it.

A man knows what to say and says it. A woman knows what not to say and says it.

A statistician is a guy who draws a mathematically precise line from an unwarranted assumption to a foregone conclusion.

A Minneapolis man defines experience as "compulsory education."

Husband to wife: "I'm telling you—one more TV dinner and you better look for a new sponsor!"

An expert is someone who knows no more than you do but has it better organized and uses slides.

The joys of motherhood are what a woman experiences every day, when the kids are finally in bed.

When a woman insists that she doesn't repeat gossip, she means you'd better listen carefully the first time.

Cosmetics are beauty products used by teen-agers to make them look older sooner, and by their mothers to make them look younger longer.

She has a keen sense of rumor.

A high class plumber is a drain surgeon.

A reckless driver is seldom wreckless for very long.

Every husband knows: Clothes break the man.

A mirage is a place where Arabs keep their camels at night.

Visitors always make us happy—some when they come and others when they go.

There's always free cheese in a mousetrap, but you never saw a happy mouse there.

274

There was a time when a fool and his money were soon parted. Now it happens to everybody.

A man has arrived when he can be as cranky at the office as at the breakfast table.

Their unhappiness is due to illness—they're sick of each other.

A husband is a man who wishes he had as much fun when he is out as his wife thinks he does.

Sadly we must admit that the various names of perfumes suggest that virtue doesn't make scents.

A gossip is one who burns the scandal at both ends.

A bore is someone who is here today and here tomorrow.

Matrimony is the splice of life.

Retirement is the time of life when you stop lying about your age and start lying about the house.

Seat belts are nothing new. Grandfather had one hanging by the bathroom sink.

A man begins cutting his wisdom teeth the first time he bites off more than he can chew.

Cosmetics are a woman's means for keeping men from reading between the lines.

One woman's definition of retirement: "Twice as much husband on half as much money."

A woman never knows what she can do until she cries.

The reason many people don't live within their income is that they don't consider that living.

She had a unique luminosity in her eyes that comes to a girl with her first suitor and to a kitten with its first mouse.

One way to reduce blood pressure is to live within your income.

Some politicians thank profits are wicked, but they certainly meet the payroll better than deficits.

If most of us practiced what we preach, we would certainly be kept awfully, awfully busy.

Probate Judge: One with will power.

When a woman says she won't be a minute, she's usually right.

The trouble with school drop-outs is not that they can't see the handwriting on the wall, but they can't read it.

Definition of a tired Santa Claus: A Beat-Nick.

The world really isn't any worse. It's just that the news coverage is so much better.

Old confidence men never die, they just steal away.

Now that I've taught my youngster the value of a dollar, he wants more money!

Chivalry is the attitude of a man towards a strange woman.

"There was something about you I liked," said the glamour girl, "but you spent it."

Intuition is what enables a woman to contradict her husband before he says anything.

People who live in glass houses make interesting neighbors.

Folk singer: A guy who sings through his nose by ear.

Good after-dinner speaker: One who pops in, pops off and then pops out.

A snob is a person who wants to know only the people who don't want to know him.

Sign on a bulletin board in front of a church: Come early and get a back seat.

Wife, waltzing into house with new fur coat on, to husband: "Well, I've got my anti-freeze!"

I think dentists have more faith than anybody. It's a miracle that more of them don't get their fingers bitten off.

The average husband prefers a clothes horse to a nag.

The children's hour is any time they're on the telephone.

People who complain that Americans spend more money for liquor than they do for education don't realize what you can learn at a cocktail party!

It's a small world until you start chasing your wind-blown hat down the street.

Many a child who watches television for hours will go down in history—not to mention arithmetic, English and geography.

"Where there's a will," there are always outstretched hands.

Taxes are just like golf. You drive your heart out for the green, and then end up in a hole.

If the postman rings more than twice these days, there's probably a cent due on one of your letters.

In politics, people are friends or enemies. In business they are all customers.

An echo is pretty accurate, but it doesn't contribute much that is new.

He who keeps his mind on his work, goes ahead; he who keeps his work on his mind, goes nuts.

Good judgment comes from experience, and experience— well, that comes from poor judgment.

Education is what one has left after subtracting what is forgotten from what one has learned.

Lack of pep is often mistaken for patience.

Good times is the period when you accumulate debts you're unable to pay in bad times.

It's too bad so many people have such a bright future behind them.

Some say that even in the Stone Age when a woman wrote down her age, she chiseled a little.

Nowadays the earth revolves on its taxes.

Two thirds of promotion is always motion.

Before long the term, "A dollar to a doughnut" may be about right.

The older we get the farther we had to walk to school in our youth.

He's the kind of politician that shakes your hand before election and your confidence after.

An open mind is fine—if it isn't accompanied by an open mouth.

Men, like boats, toot loudest, when they are lost in a fog.

Everyone makes mistakes, but persons give them assistance.

A narrow-minded man doesn't hold opinions—opinions hold him.

Aunt Hannah says she needs a soap powder that will prevent a telephone ring in the bathtub.

Modesty: The art of encouraging people to find out for themselves how important you are.

Most of us carry our own stumbling block around with us; we camouflage it with a hat.

The best social security number you can have is the number on the front door of a home you have worked to own.

Tranquilizing pills will help you to stop worrying about inflation. But they have gone up in price, too.

There's one thing you can say for the men in charge of the government—they're running it like nobody's business.

Alacrity: What a small boy rises with on Christmas morning.

Benjamin Franklin may have discovered electricity but the man who invented the meter made all the money.

Bars are something which if you go into too many of, you are apt to come out singing a few of, and maybe land behind some of.

Did you hear about the father who fainted when his son asked for the garage keys and came out with the lawn mower?

A woman never admits she has lost an argument. She just thinks she has failed to make her position clear.

Doing nothing is better than being busy doing nothing.

Tomorrow: One of the greatest labor-saving inventions of all time.

To err is human. To blame it on the other party is politics.

Everything comes to those who wait—on themselves.

Money cannot buy happiness. On the other hand, happiness cannot buy money.

According to American standards you're a "success" if you're making money enough to meet obligations you wouldn't have if you didn't make so much money.

Electric toothbrush owners are advised to brush twice a day and see their electrician twice a year.

We live in a free country where a man may say what he thinks—if he isn't afraid of his wife, his neighbors, or his boss, and if he's sure it won't hurt his business or his reputation.

There's nothing like a dish towel for wiping the contented look off a husband's face.

Space travel is going to make it easy to separate the men from us cowards.

An argument is when two people are trying to get in the last word first.

Women who are too unselfish make the best wives and the worst husbands.

A careful driver is one who just saw the driver ahead of him get a traffic ticket.

Women not only have equal rights but the alimony they receive when they divorce their husbands proves that they have sequel rights.

The old-fashioned woman of today is one who tries to make one husband last a lifetime.

A good listener is usually thinking about something else.

A geneologist is a person who traces your family history as far as your money will go.

Of course the dollar goes farther today. In fact, a lot of it ends up in outer space.

In this modern world you get only what you pay too much for.

An egotist is a man who thinks as much of himself as you think of yourself.

Only a nation with a rugged Constitution could stand the abuse ours is getting these days.

Living in the past has one thing in its favor—it's cheaper.

Sometimes adult education begins with a teenage marriage.

If it goes in one ear and out the mouth, it's gossip.

What the world needs is a closer agreement on what the world needs.

Small boy's definition of a conscience: "Something that makes you tell your mother before your sister does."

The honeymoon is over when your wife starts complaining about the noise you make when you are getting breakfast.

The man who stands constantly on his dignity is located on a mighty slippery spot.

Things are pretty well evened up in this world. Other people's troubles are not as bad as yours, but their children are a lot worse.

Sympathy seems to be the best gift for the man who has everything.

Putting your best foot forward at least keeps it out of your mouth.

A man may have more money than brains—but not for long.

Electricity is a wonderful thing. If we didn't have it, we couldn't see television except by candlelight.

When both the speaker and the audience are confused, the speech is "profound."

The term "rush hour" is that time of day when a motorist travels the shortest distance possible in the longest possible time.

Almost everyone knows the difference between right and wrong, but some hate to make the decision.

The optimist always wants you to cheer up when things are going his way.

Inflation: When those who saved for a rainy day get soaked.

If you look like your passport photo, you aren't well enough to travel.

Modern prosperity means two cars in the garage, a boat in the driveway, and a note due at the bank.

Arthritis: Twinges in the hinges.

Most automobiles keep owners pretty well strapped even without seat belts.

Too many people are ready to carry the stool when there's a piano to move.

Everybody likes a good loser—provided it is the other team.

Many a man works hard to keep the wolf from the door; then his daughter grows up and brings one right into the house.

The trouble with a fellow who talks too fast is that he is liable to say something that he hasn't even thought of yet.

Advice to the thin: Don't eat fast. Advice to the fat: Don't eat; fast.

Some folks think that traveling around in the best circles makes them big wheels.

A man owes it to himself to become successful; after that, he owes it to the Bureau of Internal Revenue.

Some folks think they are busy when they are only confused.

Life is like a game of tennis; the player who serves well seldom loses.

A good listener is not only popular everywhere, but after awhile he knows something.—*Wilson Mizner*

Evening is that period when people do the craziest things to keep from going to bed.

Said the backyard gardener: "I'm growing beans, peas, tomatoes, squash, and tired."

A pedigreed animal is any farm animal that has been run down by a motorist.

Fish grow faster than any other living thing. In fact, the average fish that is caught grows about six inches every time the story is told.

People have too much to live on, and too little to live for.

Remember the good old days when a juvenile delinquent was a youngster who owed a few cents on an overdue library book?

When a day is done you frequently discover that not much else is.

Courage is something you always have until you need it.

We do our best talking on saving money when we haven't any.

It is advisable to be careful when you give advice—somebody might take it.

Hard work is nothing more than an accumulation of easy things you didn't do when you should have.

You probably wouldn't worry quite so much about what other people think of you if you could know how seldom they really do.

A tongue twister is a group of words that suddenly get your tang all tongueled up.

The strongest words usually are used in the weakest arguments.

And why are we so anxious to conquer outer space when we haven't even solved the parking problem yet?

A well-known Hollywood actress was recently described as a good housekeeper—every time she's divorced she keeps the house.

Nonchalance is the ability to look like an owl when you've acted like a jackass.

Columbus took a trip on borrowed money and established the custom on our shore.

No one can tell you how to save money like the person who hasn't any.

The smart husband never asks who is boss around the house.

One of the greatest changes in our way of life of late is incorporated in the conversion of the old saying that "You can't take it with you" to "You can't keep it while you're here."

Middle-age: When a woman takes her high school annual out of the bookcase and hides it where the children can't find it.

There is nothing wrong with the younger generation that the older generation hasn't outgrown.

The remarkable thing about college reunions is that your classmates have gotten so stout and bald they hardly recognize you.

The surest way to knock the chip off a fellow's shoulder is by patting him on the back.

The height of unimportance is that sensation you have when you make a mistake and nobody notices it.

Mothers who scold little boys for carrying crazy things in their pockets should look in their own handbags.

Warning: If your wife wants to learn to drive, don't stand in her way.

A chrysanthemum by any other name would be easier to spell.

The Supreme Court of the United States gives a man a right to open his wife's letters, but it doesn't give him the courage.

One should pity the blind, but it's hard to do if the rascal is the umpire.

Definition of fog: Stuff that is dangerous to drive in, especially if it is mental.

The probable reason some people get lost in thought is because it is unfamiliar territory to them.

A bargain is something you cannot use at a price you cannot resist.

Even a mosquito doesn't get a slap on the back till he starts working.

An executive is a man who can take two hours for lunch without hindering production.

Try to imagine a cracker barrel philosopher holding forth in a supermarket.

You may not know all the answers, but you probably won't be asked all the questions, either.

Nothing is as easy as it looks, except spending money.

A sign of the times: An old-timer is one who used to drop the boy off at school on his way to work. Now he has a boy who drops him off at work on his way to school.

Then there was the fellow who said the only reason he was lazy was because it kept him from getting so tired.

They say you can't take it with you, but have you ever tried to travel very far without it?

More children are spoiled because parents can't spank Grandma.

'Twas the night before Christmas, and all through the house, not a creature was stirring—they had an electric mixer.

Do it tomorrow—you've made enough mistakes today.

Another thing so simple a child can operate it is a grandparent.

"Practice does not make a lawyer perfect," says a famous judge. But enough of it will make him rich.

People who cough never go to the doctor. They go to the theatres.

A business is too big when it takes a week for gossip to go from one end of the office to the other.

CHAPTER 7

UNUSUAL QUOTATIONS

Temper

Keep your temper. Do not quarrel with an angry person but give him a soft answer. It is commanded by the Holy Writ, and, furthermore, it makes him madder than anything else you could say.—*Anonymous*

Indignation

Your own wrath as opposed to the shocking bad temper of others.—*Anonymous*

Immortality

The truest end of Life is to know that Life never ends. . . . For tho' Death be a Dark Passage, it leads to Immortality, and that's Recompense enough for suffering of it.—*William Penn*

Taking Sides

One should never take sides in anything. Taking sides is the beginning of sincerity, and ernestness follows shortly afterwards, and the human being becomes a bore.—*Oscar Wilde*

Language

Drawing on fine command of language, I said nothing.
—*Robert Benchley*

England and America are two countries separated by the same language.—*George Bernard Shaw*

Gentleman

A gentleman is one who never strikes a woman without provocation.—*H. L. Mencken*

It is the final test of a gentleman—his respect for those who can be of no possible service to him.—*William Lyon Phelps*

Money

I don't like money actually, but it quiets my nerves.
—*Joe Louis*

He had so much money that he could afford to look poor.
—*Edgar Wallace*

When a fellow says, "It ain't the money but the principle of the thing," it's the money.—*Frank McKinney Hubbard*

Think

If you make people think they're thinking, they'll love you; but if you really make them think, they'll hate you.
—*Don Marquis*

Indiana

I come from Indiana, the home of more first-rate second-class men than any state in the Union.—*Thomas R. Marshall*

Fame

His utter incapacity and his gift for the resounding phrase assured him of splendid destiny.—*Georges Courtilines*

Small Inner Voice

Conscience is a small inner voice that frequently doesn't speak your language.—*Anonymous*

Conceit

Conceit: God's gift to little men.—*Bruce Barton*

He was like a cock who thought the sun had risen to hear him crow.—*George Eliot*

Sincerity

A little sincerity is a dangerous thing, and a great deal of it is absolutely fatal.—*Oscar Wilde*

History

History books which contain no lies are extremely dull. —*Anatole France*

Predicament

Small boy: "If I'm noisy they give me a spanking . . . and if I'm quiet they take my temperature."—*Anonymous*

Committee

If Moses had been a committee, the Israelites would still be in Egypt.—*J. B. Hughes*

Conscience

I have a terrible conscience—it doesn't keep me from doing things; it just keeps me from enjoying them.—*Anonymous*

Conscience: The inner voice which warns us that someone may be looking.—*H. L. Mencken*

Children

Children are natural mimics—they act like their parents in spite of every attempt to teach them good manners.

—Anonymous

By the time the youngest children have learned to keep the house tidy, the oldest grandchildren are on hand to tear it to pieces again.—*Christopher Morley*

Children are a great comfort in your old age—and they help you to reach it faster, too.—*Lionel M. Kaufman*

Don't take up a man's time talking about the smartness of your children; he wants to talk to you about the smartness of his children.—*Edgar Watson Howe*

Before I got married I had six theories about bringing up children; now I have six children, and no theories.

—*Lord Rochester*

Idleness

It is impossible to enjoy idling thoroughly unless one has plenty of work to do.—*Jerome K. Jerome*

Woman

Woman: The last thing civilized by man.

It is not true that woman was made from man's rib; she was really made from his funny bone.—*James Matthew Barrie*

Age

As soon as a man acquires fairly good sense, it is said he is an old fogey.—*E. W. Howe*

Everything I know I learned after I was thirty.

—*Georges Clemenceau*

A diplomat is a man who always remembers a woman's birthday but never remembers her age.—*Robert Frost*

Adversity

I'll say this for adversity: people seem to be able to stand it, and that's more than I can say for prosperity.

—*Frank McKinney Hubbard*

Adversity is the state in which a man most easily becomes acquainted with himself, being especially free from admirers then.—*Samuel Johnson*

Civilization

It needs civilization, it needs second thoughts, to realize that Napoleon and Caesar and Alexander are not really the highest types of humanity, that war-making is not a glory, but a crime.—*Gilbert Murray*

The path of civilization is paved with tin cans.

—Albert Hubbard

Happiness

If ignorance is bliss, why aren't there more happy people? —*Anonymous*

The only way to avoid being miserable is not to have enough leisure to wonder whether you are happy or not.

—George Bernard Shaw

Happiness is the perpetual possession of being well deceived.—*Jonathan Swift*

Truth

It is hard to believe that a man is telling the truth when you know that you would lie if you were in his place.

—Henry L. Mencken

The devil is the father of lies, but he neglected to patent the idea, and the business now suffers from competition.

—Josh Billings

With a man, a lie is a last resort; with women, it's First Aid.—*Gellett Burgess*

I do not mind lying, but I hate inaccuracy.—*Samuel Butler*

Convalescence

I enjoy convalescence; it is the part that makes the illness worthwhile.—*George Bernard Shaw*

Farm

The first recipe to farm well is to be rich.—*Sydney Smith*

Faults

We are always hard on our own faults in others; we know how inexcusable they are.—*I. Compton-Burnett*

Lie

A lie with a purpose is one of the worst kind, and the most profitable.—*Finley Peter Dunne*

Culture

She invariably was first over the fence in the mad pursuit of culture.—*George Ade*

Hat

Her hat is a creation that will never go out of style; it will just look ridiculous year after year.—*Fred Allen*

Critic

I never read a book before reviewing it; it prejudices one so.—*Sydney Smith*

Conversation

Macaulay has occasional flashes of silence that make his conversation perfectly delightful.—*Sydney Smith*

Clock

When a man retires and time is no longer a matter of urgent importance, his colleagues generally present him with a clock.—*R. C. Sheriff*

Importance

It was prettily devised of Aesop, the fly sat upon the axletree of the chariot wheel, and said, "What a dust do I raise."
—*Francis Bacon*

Youth

I am not young enough to know everything.
                                    —*James Matthew Barrie*

Beware of what you wish for in youth, for in middle age you will surely achieve it.—*Johann von Goethe*

Repartee

Repartee is an insult with its dress suit on.—*Anonymous*

Romance

To love oneself is the beginning of a lifelong romance.
                                    —*Oscar Wilde*

Philosophy

Philosophy: Unintelligible answers to insoluble problems.
—*Henry Adams*

Best People

Early to bed and early to rise, and you'll meet very few of our best people.—*George Ade*

Soprano

She was a town-and-counary soprano of the kind often used for augmenting the grief at a funeral.—*George Ade*

Features

Her features did not seem to know the value of teamwork. —*George Ade*

Genius

When a true genius appears in the world, you may know him by this sign, that the dunces are all in confederacy against him.—*Jonathan Swift*

You may have genius. The contrary is, of course, probable. —*Oliver Wendell Holmes*

I have nothing to declare except my genius.—*Oscar Wilde*

Property

Thieves respect property; they merely wish the property to become their property that they may more perfectly respect it.

Illness

I've just learned about his illness; let's hope it's nothing trivial.—*Irvin Shrewsbury Cobb*

Advice

In those days he was wiser than he is now; he used frequently to take my advice.—*Winston Churchill*

Funny

Everything is funny that happens to somebody else.
Collie Knox

Actor

You can pick out actors by the glazed look that comes into their eyes when the conversation wanders away from themselves.—*Michael Wilding*

Extravagance

An extravagance is anything you buy that is of no earthly use to your wife.—*Franklin P. Jones*

Wife to husband: "All right, I admit I like to spend money . . . but name one other extravagance."—*Anonymous*

Where He Shines

I do most of my work sitting down: that's where I shine. —*Robert Benchley*

Save Some

Work is the greatest thing in the world, so we should always save some of it for tomorrow.—*Don Herold*

Income

Live within your income, even if you have to borrow money to do so.—*Josh Billings*

Neighbors

The Bible tells us to love our neighbors, and also to love our enemies; probably because they are generally the same people.—*Gilbert Keith Chesterton*

Optimism

Optimism: The noble temptation to see too much in everything.—*Gilbert Keith Chesterton*

Ego

Talk to a man about himself and he will listen for hours.
—*Benjamin Disraeli*

I've given up reading books; I find it takes my mind off myself.—*Oscar Levant*

Psychologist

Psychologist: A man who, when a beautiful girl enters the room, watches everybody else.—*Bruce Patterson*

Diplomacy

Diplomacy is the art of letting someone have your way.
—*Daniele Vare*

Admiration

Admiration: Our polite recognition of another's resemblance to ourselves.—*Ambrose Bierce*

Peace of Mind

Nothing contributes more to peace of mind than to have no opinions whatever.—*G. C. Lichtenberg*

Achievement

Periods of tranquility are seldom prolific of creative achievement. Mankind has to be stirred up.

—*Alfred North Whitehead*

Quiet

It is difficult to keep quiet if you have nothing to do.
—*Schopenhauer*

Bachelor

A bachelor is one who thinks one can live as cheap as two.
—*Eleanor S. J. Ridley*

All reformers are bachelors.—*George Moore*

Modest

I was a modest, good-humored boy; it is Oxford that has
made me insufferable.—*Max Beerbohm*

Ignorance

He was distinguished for ignorance; for he had only one
idea and that was wrong.—*Benjamin Disraeli*

Journalism

What is the difference between journalism and literature?
Oh! Journalism is unreadable, and literature is not read.
That is all.—*Oscar Wilde*

Author

After being turned down by numerous publishers, he decided to write for posterity.—*George Ade*

It took me fifteen years to discover I had no talent for
writing, but I couldn't give it up because by that time I was too
famous.—*Robert Benchley*

Infinitive

Word has somehow got around that the split infinitive is
always wrong. This is of a piece with the outworn notion that
it is always wrong to strike a lady.—*Robert Benchley*

Politics

Politics is the gentle art of getting votes from the poor and campaign funds from the rich by promising to protect each from the other.—*Anonymous*

Democracy

Democracy is the recurrent suspicion that more than half of the people are right more than half of the time.—*E. B. White*

Ideal Voice

The ideal voice for radio may be defined as having no substance, no sex, no owner, and a message of importance to every housewife.—*Harry V. Wade*

Science

In everything that relates to science, I am a whole encyclopedia behind the rest of the world.—*Charles Lamb*

Impromptu Speeches

It is an inflexible rule of mine not to make impromptu speeches without good warning . . . As Lord Goddard said, they are not worth the paper they are written on.—*E. Horsfall Turner*

Work

Work expands so as to fill the time available for its completion. ('Parkinson's Law.')—*C. Northcote Parkinson*

I like work; it fascinates me. I can sit and look at it for hours.—*Jerome K. Jerome*

I go on working for the same reason that a hen goes on laying eggs.—*H. L. Mencken*

Words

My wife and I had words—but I never got to use mine.
—*Fibber McGee*

Experience

Experience is a school where a man learns what a big fool
he has been.—*Josh Billings*

Experience is a name everyone gives to their mistakes.
—*Oscar Wilde*

Example

Few things are harder to put up with than the annoyance
of a good example.—*Mark Twain*

We learn from experience. A man never wakes up his
second baby just to see it smile.—*Grace Williams*

Speech

If you don't say anything, you won't be called on to repeat
it.—*Calvin Coolidge*

Even the weariest river.

Winds somewhere safe to sea.—*A. C. Swinburne*

Half the world is composed of people who have something
to say and can't, and the other half who have nothing to say and
keep on saying it.—*Robert Frost*

No man would listen to you talk if he didn't know it was
his turn next.—*Edgar Watson Howe*

It usually takes me more than three weeks to prepare a
good impromptu speech.—*Mark Twain*

Wife

A man likes his wife to be just clever enough to compre-
hend his cleverness, and just stupid enough to admire it.

—*Israel Zangwill*

Recession

Recession is a period in which you tighten up your belt. In a depression you have no belt to tighten up—and when you have no pants to hold up, it's a panic.—*Anonymous*

Middle Age

Middle age: When you begin to exchange your emotions for symptoms.—*Irvin S. Cobb*

Paris

Paris is a city of gaieties and pleasures where four fifths of the inhabitants die of grief.—*Nicholas Chamfort*

Fashion

Change in fashion is the tax which the industry of the poor levies on the vanity of the rich.—*Nicholas Chamfort*

Poverty

No man should commend poverty unless he is poor.
—*St. Bernard*

Weather

What dreadful hot weather we have! It keeps one in a continual state of inelegance.—*Jane Austen*

Education

Education is an admirable thing, but it is well to remember from time to time that nothing that is worth knowing can be taught.—*Oscar Wilde*

A Balliol education gives a man a tranquil sense of effortless superiority.—*The late Lord Oxford and Asquith*

Sister

Two are better than one, but the man who said that did not know my sisters.—*Samuel Butler*

Politician

An honest politician is one who when he is bought will stay bought.—*Simon Cameron*

Press Agents

All press agents belong to a club of which Ananias is the honorary president.—*John Kendrick Bangs*

Opinion Surveys

Opinion Surveys: People who don't matter reporting on opinions that do matter.—*John A. Lincoln*

Tolerance

Tolerance: Another word for indifference.
—*W. Somerset Maugham*

Patience

Patience: A minor form of despair disguised as a virtue.
—*Ambrose Bierce*

Consult

Consult: To seek another's approval of a course already decided on.—*Ambrose Bierce*

Vice

Vice is a creature of such hideous mien that the more you see it, the better you like it.—*Finley Peter Dunne*

Fanatic

Fanaticism consists in redoubling your effort when you have forgotten your aim.—*George Santayana*

Life

Life is a jest, and all things show it,

I thought so once, and now I know it.—*Thomas Gay*

Life is no brief candle to me. It is a sort of splendid torch that I have got hold of for the moment.—*George Bernard Shaw*

To get the whole world out of bed.

And washed and dressed and warmed and fed,

To work, and back to bed again,

Believe me, Saul, costs worlds of pain.—*John Masefield*

Everyone has some useful purpose in life—if only to serve as a horrible example.—*Anonymous*

Humility

Humility is the first of the virtues—for other people.
—*Oliver Wendell Holmes*

Thought

A "new thinker," when studied closely, is merely a man who does not know what other people have thought.
—*Frank Moore Colby*

Books

Isn't it strange that I who have written only unpopular books should be such a popular fellow?—*Albert Einstein*

Never lend books, for no one ever returns them; the only books I have in my library are books that other folk have lent me.—*Anatole France*

It really deserves the praise, whatever that praise may be worth, of being the best book ever written by any man on the wrong side of the question of which he was profoundly ignorant. —*Thomas Babington Macaulay*

Conviction

The difference between a conviction and a prejudice is that you can explain a conviction without getting angry.

—*Anonymous*

Reason

Reasoning with a child is fine, if you can reach the child's reason without destroying your own.—*John Mason Brown*

Social Life

It was one of those parties where you cough twice before you speak, and then decide not to say it after all.

—*P. G. Wodehouse*

Mind

He discloses the working of a mind to which incoherence lends an illusion of profundity.—*T. De Vere White*

Travel

In America there are two classes of travel—first class, and with children.—*Robert Benchley*

She went up the Nile as far as the first crocodile.

—*Samuel Butler*

Courage

Courage is not freedom from fear: it is being afraid and going on.—*Anonymous*

The essence of courage is not that your heart should not quake, but that nobody else should know that it does.

— *E. F. Benson*

Luck

I am a great believer in luck, and I find the harder I work the more I have of it.—*Stephen Leacock*

If anything lucky happens to you, don't fail to go and tell it to your friends in order to annoy them.—*Count Montroud*

Soap and Education

Soap and education are not as sudden as a massacre, but they are more deadly in the long run.—*Mark Twain*

Government

Bad officials are elected by good citizens who do not vote.
—*George Jean Nathan*

Bored

People always get tired of one another. I grow tired of myself whenever I am left alone for ten minutes, and I am certain that I am fonder of myself than anyone can be of another person.—*George Bernard Shaw*

Alexandre Dumas, pere, was asked after a dinner party: "Well, how did it go?"

"Not too well," he replied. "If I hadn't been there myself, I should have been bored to death."

Heredity

Heredity is an omnibus in which all our ancestors ride, and every now and then one of them puts his head out and embarrasses us.—*Oliver Wendell Holmes*

America

America is the country where you buy a lifetime supply of aspirin for one dollar, and use it up in two weeks.

—*John Barrymore*

Scandal

Scandal is gossip made tedious by morality.—*Oscar Wilde*

Insomnia

He had insomnia so bad that he couldn't sleep when he was working.—*Arthur Baer*

Insomnia: A contagious disease often transmitted from babies to parents.—*Shannon Fife*

Wealth

If a man is wise, he gets rich, and if he gets rich, he gets foolish, or his wife does.—*Finley Peter Dunne*

Florida

Florida's all right if you can keep from catching a sailfish and going to the expense of having it mounted.

—*Frank McKinney Hubbard*

Happiness or Power

"If I could but show you the cabbages which I have planted here with my own hands, you would not urge me to relinquish the joys of happiness for the pursuit of power."

—*Diocletian (to his former co-emperor Maximilian)*

The Wrong Society

We must beware of trying to build a society in which nobody counts for anything except a politician or an official, a society where enterprise gains no reward, and thrift no privileges.—*Winston Churchill*

New York

There is more sophistication and less sense in New York than anywhere else on the globe.—*Don Herold*

Celebrity

Celebrity: A man who works all his life to become famous enough to be recognized—then goes around in dark glasses so no one will know who he is.—*Earl Wilson*

Night School

"Whom are you?" said he, for he had been to night school. —*George Ade*

Art

That woman's art-jargon tires me . . . she's so fond of talking of certain pictures as "growing on one," as though they were a sort of fungus.—*Saki*

Judge

A judge is a law student who marks his own examination papers.—*H. L. Mencken*

Wedding

Nobody enjoys a wedding but the bride's mother—she likes a good cry.—*R. W. Kauffman*

Literature

Once (women) read Baudelaire. Now it is the Consumers' Guide. Once they wrote poetry. Now it's the laundry list.
—*Adlai E. Stevenson*

Tax Return

Some day a tax return may contain only three questions:

1. How much money have you got?
2. Where is it?
3. How soon can you get at it?—*Anonymous*

Calamities

Calamities are of two kinds: misfortune to ourselves, and good fortune to others.—*Ambrose Bierce*

Statesman

A conservative is a statesman who is enamored of existing evils, as distinguished from the liberal who wishes to replace them with others.—*Ambrose Bierce*

Discussion

Discussion: A method of confirming others in their errors.
—*Ambrose Bierce*

Acquaintance

Acquaintance: A person whom we know well enough to borrow from, but not well enough to lend to.—*Ambrose Bierce*

Circus

If a circus is half as good as it smells, it's a great show.
—*Fred Allen*

Good Spirits

All the guests were in good spirits and vice versa.

—Anonymous

Fault

She's generous to a fault—if it's her own.—*Arthur Baer*

Dull

He was dull in a new way, and that made many think him great.—*Samuel Johnson*

Manuscript

Your manuscript is both good and original; but the part that is good is not original, and the part that is original is not good.—*Samuel Johnson*

Look

He gave her a look that you could have poured on a waffle. —*Ring Lardner*

Gratitude

Gratitude is merely a secret hope of greater favors.

—Francois de La Rochefoucauld

Misfortune

In the misfortune of our best friends we find something which is not displeasing to us.—*Francois de La Rochefoucauld*

Grammar

Everything bows to success, even grammar.—*Victor Hugo*

Egoist

Egotist: A person of low taste, more interested in himself than in me.—*Ambrose Bierce*

President

When I was a boy I was told anybody could become President; I'm beginning to believe it.—*Clarence Darrow*

Credit

Credit: A person who can't pay, gets another person who can't pay, to guarantee that he can pay.—*Charles Dickens*

Lawyers

If there were no bad people, there would be no good lawyers.—*Charles Dickens*

I was never ruined but twice: once when I lost a lawsuit, and once when I won one.—*Voltaire*

Sing

I am saddest when I sing; so are those who hear me; they are sadder even than I am.—*Artemus Ward*

Recognize

I beg your pardon, I didn't recognize you—I've changed a lot.—*Oscar Wilde*

Inexperience

In America, the young are always ready to give to those who are older than themselves the full benefits of their inexperience.—*Oscar Wilde*

Success

The secret of success in life is known only to those who have not succeeded.—*John Churton Collins*

I dread success. To have succeeded is to have finished one's business on earth.—*George Bernard Shaw*

Success may go to one's head but the stomach is where it gets in its worst work.—*Frank McKinney Hubbard*

Be nice to people on your way up because you'll meet them on your way down.—*Wilson Mizner*

All you need in this life is ignorance and confidence, and then success is sure.—*Mark Twain*

There's always something about your success that displeases even your best friends.—*Mark Twain*

Examinations

In examinations the foolish ask questions that the wise cannot answer.—*Oscar Wilde*

Wishing

Many of us spend half our time wishing for things we could have if we didn't spend half our time wishing.

—*Alexander Woollcott*

Theater

The scenery in the play was beautiful, but the actors got in front of it.—*Alexander Woollcott*

Troubles

I am an old man and have known a great many troubles, but most of them never happened.—*Mark Twain*

Compliment

I can live for two months on a good compliment.

—*Mark Twain*

Criticism

I like criticism, but it must be my way.—*Mark Twain*

Brotherhood

In all my travels the thing that has impressed me the most is the universal brotherhood of man—what there is of it.

—*Mark Twain*

Diamonds

Let us not be too particular; it is better to have old second-hand diamonds than none at all.—*Mark Twain*

Music

Wagner's music is better than it sounds.—*Mark Twain*

Food

Part of the secret of success in life is to eat what you like and let the food fight it out inside.—*Mark Twain*

Civilized

I know I am among civilized men because they are fighting so savagely.—*Voltaire*

Greatness

We are both great men, but I have succeeded better in keeping it a profound secret than he has.—*Edgar Wilson Nye*

Liberty

There should be more in American liberty than the privilege we enjoy of insulting the President with impunity.

—*Austin O'Malley*

Question

He admits that there are two sides to every question—his own and the wrong side.—*Channing Pollock*

Worry

Worry is a morbid anticipation of events which never happen.—*Russell Green*

Modern Art

One reassuring thing about modern art is that things can't be as bad as they are painted.—*M. Walthall Jackson*

Toy

The child had every toy his father wanted.

—*Robert E. Whitten*

Dream

A child, awakened out of a deep sleep, expressed all the crying babies and all the weeping idealists in the world. "Oh, dear," he said, "I have lost my place in my dream."

—*Lincoln Steffens*

The boy gathers materials for a temple, and when he is thirty concludes to build a woodshed.—*Henry David Thoreau*

Taxation

Colbert said that the art of taxation consists in so plucking the goose as to procure the greatest quantity of feathers with the least amount of hissing.—*W. Smart*

Dog

The great pleasure of a dog is that you may make a fool of yourself with him and not only will he not scold you, but he will make a fool of himself too.—*Samuel Butler*

Newspaper

A newspaper is a circulating library with high blood pressure.—*Arthur Baer*

Congregation

A congregation who can't afford to pay a clergyman enough wants a missionary more than they do a clergyman.

—*Josh Billings*

Listener

A good listener is not only popular everywhere, but after a while he knows something.—*Wilson Mizner*

Dinner

After a good dinner one forgives everyone—even relations.
—*Oscar Wilde*

This was a good enough dinner, to be sure; but it was not a dinner to ask a man to.—*Dr. Samuel Johnson*

Death

Sleep is, in fine, so like death, I dare not trust it without my prayers.—*Sir Thomas Browne*

Wisdom

I do not believe in the collective wisdom of individual ignorance.—*Thomas Carlyle*

Man

Man . . . like an angry ape
Plays such fantastic tricks before high heaven
As makes the angels weep . . . —*William Shakespeare*

If a man is only a little lower than the angels, the angels should reform.—*Mary Wilson Little*

Everyone is as God made him, and often a great deal worse. —*Miguel de Cervantes*

Marriage

Marriage, which make two one, is a lifelong struggle to discover which is that one.—*Anonymous*

A wise woman will always let her husband have her way. —*R. B. Sheridan*

Successful marriage results when you treat all disasters as incidents and none of the incidents as disasters.

—*Harold Nicolson*

Overheard: "I married her because we have so many faults in common."—*Anonymous*

Marriage is one long conversation, chequered by disputes. —*R. L. Stevenson*

Married life ain't so bad after you get so you can eat the things your wife likes.—*Frank McKinney Hubbard*

Health

Never tell people how you are: they don't want to know. —*Johann von Goethe*

He is remarkably well, considering that he has been remarkably well for so many years.—*Sydney Smith*